Nobody will ever kill me

Nobody will ever kill me

Mbu Maloni

Written with Lutz van Dijk

UNIVERSITY OF KWAZULU-NATAL PRESS

Published in 2011 by University of KwaZulu-Natal Press
Private Bag X01
Scottsville 3209
South Africa
Email: books@ukzn.ac.za
Website: www.ukznpress.co.za

ISBN: 978-1-86914-217-9

Editor: Elana Bregin
Proofreader: Juliet Haw
Typesetter: Patricia Comrie
Cover design: Flying Ant Designs
Cover photographs: Chad Chapman

Typeset in Gentium Book Basic

Printed and bound by Interpak Books, Pietermaritzburg

This book is dedicated

to my friend

Abongile 'Atie' Rwanqa

(1994–2010)

who was brutally murdered at the age of fifteen
by another boy of seventeen – for no reason.

Asoze ndiku libale –
I will never forget you, Atie!

Mbu Maloni
Masiphumelele, Cape Town, South Africa

Contents

1

Long ago: The baby I never was
Kudala: Azange ndibe lusana

What does one remember first in life? Maybe a smell, a voice, the warmth of the skin of your mom? I try to remember and I can't.

The first thing I remember is something I am ashamed of. Maybe that's why I don't want to remember. I want to forget. I don't have a first nice memory in life. So, I actually don't want to be reminded of when I was small, when I was even more tiny than most other babies. That, at least, is what I heard many years later from my Auntie Nompumelelo, the one I loved more than my own mom.

It's painful that even she has rejected me now. That even she does not greet me on the street anymore . . .

But I promised myself to be honest with this book. I want to write it to become stronger. So, I have to be honest. Even if the truth is not nice.

Like – when I was a baby. I was not only tiny, much too small for my age; maybe I just did not want to be born at all. Because my mom is an alcoholic. Because I did not know how much I would have to struggle after birth. I probably wanted to stay inside my mom's tummy. There, it must have been warm and safe – and, probably, I was never hungry. But maybe not even this is true – maybe I was afraid already in her womb. Can an unborn baby hear the shouting of the outside world? Is an unborn baby hungry when the mother is not eating but mostly just drinking?

Okay, enough uncertain thoughts. My first memory: me crying. All the time. Crying, crying, crying. And nobody comforting me. Nobody even looking at me. Let alone looking after me. So – I kept crying; crying, crying, crying. What a silly first memory of life.

My name, Mbu, is a short version of *Mbuyiseli*, which means in isiXhosa *the one who returns something.*

I once asked my mom why she gave me this name. She said: 'I never got anything from life . . . I hope to get something back from my children one day . . . maybe from you.' She was sober when she said that and I almost wanted to say: yes, Mom, one day I want to give you a better life. But then I hesitated. And finally I did not say a word. Because I thought: Mom, how can I give something back when I have never really received much from you? When I was hungry so many times; when I was alone so many times; when I was cold so many times.

Except for my first school uniform . . . that I will never forget. You bought me this yellow shirt, grey short pants and a pair of shiny black shoes. All new stuff. You made me so happy and proud that day! So yes, one day, when I earn my own money, I will give you back something. But only if you stop drinking, Mom. I don't care about your boyfriend. But I don't want you to use my money for drinking.

So, when my mom said that to me, about getting something back, I did not answer her. I kept silent. Next to crying, I was silent. First lesson in life: learn to control yourself. Don't cry – and shut up. Be quiet. Don't talk. It will only create trouble. Adults always know better. Adults, generally, don't listen anyhow. So, what's the sense of talking? Of sharing what you think, what you feel, what you dream of, what you are longing for?

Maybe you can share something with a friend. But not with your family. Not with your mother. And certainly not with the men she brings home. Shut up. Be quiet. Don't cry. Put a neutral face on. A mask. That's good. Then nobody can judge you easily. Even if they think you are stupid, because you don't talk. Don't worry. Just shut up.

That's the way I thought for most of my life. I don't think that way anymore. I've started to talk a bit in the place where I am now. Kind of the first home I've ever had. If home means – a safe place, where nobody will attack you. Where there is food without fighting. Where you can keep your own stuff safe and clean. Where people don't gossip about you. Where you can sleep without fear.

It was in this place that I started to write about my life. Because I know there are hundreds and thousands and millions of other kids out there who think they should shut up. Who think they are nothing. That they are just like rubbish. Dirty, hungry, stinking. It's not true! Every child wants to be somebody. Wants to be listened to. Even every baby. And here is where my story starts.

*

The first person in my life I really admired was my older brother Mavusi. Maybe I even loved him, because he was the first one who looked after me, although he was only four years older. But he was there, when we were both left behind, alone, in the shack at night while my mom was at the *shebeen*. I remember that he tried to put food in my mouth and I could not eat it yet because it was too hard; stuff like old bread. But, at least, he shared. Sometimes he hugged me when I was crying. Sometimes he beat me because he had enough of my crying. Both of these things I appreciated because it was the response of another human being.

His voice is still in my ears: '*Tula, man, tula . . .* be quiet, man!' he said, a thousand times. He was then maybe six and I was two; but maybe I never was a baby.

Sometimes my father was still around. There was a nice smell around him when he came home from work. A smell of fresh bread and cake. He worked in a bakery. And sometimes, when he was there, we had a lot of bread after days of nothing.

But my mom and him were fighting a lot. I don't know about what, as I just was too small. He never looked after me like my brother did. But it was good when he was there. My father is tall and strong and much older than my mom. I felt somehow safer when he was around, when I heard him snoring in his corner of the shack.

But suddenly he was gone. Just like that. I must have been about three then, not even four yet. I only met him again many, many years later. When I had started searching for him. Another story. For later, not yet.

So, my brother Mavusi was there. He tried to take me everywhere. To neighbours to beg for food. To his friends when he went to play with them. When I was too tired to walk he'd push me: '*Hamba, man* – go, man, go!' He never used my name but always called me 'man'. He was not strong enough to carry me as he was still small himself. Actually, he was a very skinny boy and sometimes had a bad cough.

*

One day a dog attacked us both. This was still in the early days in Masizakhe township in Graaff Reinet, which is where I was born. Maybe the dog came after us because of a small piece of bread

Mavusi had in his hand. But he refused to give it to the dog. The dog started growling and barking. It was a black dog with long hair and huge white teeth and a red tongue, and I was so afraid because the dog was much bigger than my brother. There was no adult around to help us. So I started screaming – not just crying but screaming, as loud as I could, full of panic that this dog might bite my brother and then eat him. And then, of course, me.

But Mavusi? He stood his ground. He grabbed a wooden stick with his right hand and kept the piece of bread in his left hand. And he started to shout at the dog: 'Suka, nja, suka – go away, dog!' He did not even swear at the dog. He was just shouting: 'Go away, dog!'

But suddenly the dog jumped and I closed my eyes in sheer terror. When I opened them again, the dog was growling horribly and standing over Mavusi, who lay on his back, trying to hide the small piece of bread. But the dog wasn't stupid. It was sniffing all over my brother. Finally, it grabbed his arm, and only then did Mavusi give up. He yelled in pain and threw the bread away from him. In one jump the hungry dog caught the slice and crunched it down. It then lost interest in us and just walked away . . .

My hero brother Mavusi was holding his arm up and trying to stop the bleeding by pressing the veins above the wound. I could not understand why he was not crying. He was eight at the most. He just mumbled: 'Inja esisidenge, inja elambileyo – stupid dog, hungry dog . . .' The bleeding stopped. But later in the day his arm became swollen. By the evening it looked terrible and he could not move his fingers anymore.

There was nobody at home. So, he woke me up and said: 'Masihambe siye kuMakazi Nompumelelo – let's go to Auntie Nompumelelo.' She lived not far from us and, fortunately, there was still a paraffin light burning in her shack. You could see the light through the wooden pieces and plastic sheets of her shack.

When she saw Mavusi's swollen arm, she shook her head and said: '*Asilunganga* – this is no good!' She did not even ask where our mom was, just put me on her back and took my brother by his uninjured hand. Then we walked to the taxi rank. But it was too late for any taxis to the hospital in Graaff Reinet. She decided that Mavusi's arm was too serious to be left till morning. And so we walked and walked and walked . . .

I fell asleep on her back and only woke up again when there was a strong light all around us. It was such a bright white room that at first I could hardly see anything. When my eyes got more used to the light, I realised that this must be the hospital. I don't remember much about the rest of that evening. And I don't know how we got back to Masizakhe.

The next morning, my brother had a huge white bandage around his arm and all the other kids looked at him with admiration. Mavusi told them: 'The dog bit off my arm but the doctor sewed it back again . . .' The other kids nodded their heads. Yes, we had some dangerous dogs that sometimes became very fierce. But the dogs were also beaten all the time . . . and they were hungry like us.

Sometimes I liked the dogs, especially the puppies. Once, I even brought a puppy home. But my mom just grabbed the puppy by its neck and threw it through the open door back into the street. '*Uphambene* – are you crazy, Mbu?' was all she said. I felt so sorry for that baby dog. I remember how sweet it was with its big black eyes like buttons, its tiny wagging tail and funny long ears.

*

When some of the other boys started school at our local primary school, our mom said to my brother: '*Linda*, Mavusi – you must wait! You will go next year . . . you have to look after your brother.' Mavusi never complained. But I saw that he was sad that he could not go to school. A year later our auntie insisted that he should go and gave him the used uniform of one of her older boys.

Although I missed Mavusi during the day, I was so proud of him. What a big boy he was – and how smart he looked in his uniform of green and black. Almost like a man! '*Haybo* – no,' he smiled, 'I am just Grade 1!' But to me he was big now. Not a small kid like me. While he was at school, I dreamt that one day I would also go to school. I thought that school must be a magical place, because it was only allowed for the older ones and they received magical powers at school.

For example, my brother showed me papers with small black signs on them. These signs did not make any sense to me. They did not show a door or a window, but my brother pointed to one and said: 'This means *ucango* – door!' He pointed to another line of signs and said: 'This means *ifestile* – window!' I did not understand and thought that he must have had a certain initiation of the traditional kind. But when he asked me, '*Uyaqonda* – do you understand?' I nodded my head. Of course.

*

My childhood ended sometime after my fifth birthday, around the end of Grade 2 for Mavusi. Without any warning, my mother said to us one hot morning in January: 'Mavusi, you stay here with *Gogo* . . .' *Gogo* was the old relative who sometimes used to look after us in Masizakhe. To me, my mother said: '*Siya eKapa* – we are going to Cape Town . . .'

7

It was the first time I opened my mouth in objection: '*Hayi, Mama* – please let me stay with Mavusi!' She looked at me in surprise but pretended that she did not hear my words. 'We leave at noon by bus . . .'

Much later I understood that she could not find any job anywhere in Graaff Reinet. Maybe also because of her drinking. In the bus, she said to another passenger: 'It's easy to get a job in *iKapa!*'

I've never forgotten how Mavusi came with us to the bus station. And how he stood there when the bus left. As if he was frozen. When I waved my hand, he did not wave back. He just stood there without a movement and became smaller and smaller the longer I looked back at him. Then the bus made a turn, and Mavusi disappeared.

This time, I was not crying. But it was hard not to. I bit on my lips until I could taste blood.

2

My first day at school
Isuku loku qala esikolweni

Actually, we never saw much of Cape Town on that first journey. I remember that far away, on the horizon, I could make out this huge famous mountain, called Table Mountain, because of its flat top. Our bus driver had stopped somewhere in the city to drop off passengers, but I had been asleep then and had missed it.

When my mom woke me up, we were already at our stop. We got off the bus and changed to a minibus taxi, my mother confirming with the other passengers that the taxi would go to Masiphumelele. The young woman next to us nodded her head: '*Ewe, Sisi* – it's not far from here.'

Indeed, not long after that, the taxi stopped at the entrance to another township, much smaller than the one we had come from. Only now did I ask my mother: 'Why are we here, Mom?'

'Because an uncle lives here and he's offered to rent us a shack in his backyard.'

This township looked even poorer than ours in *eRhafu* – the local name for Graaff Reinet. It was very dirty, with a lot of litter in the main road, and there wasn't even one street name to guide us. Finally, we came to a container which seemed to be serving as a day clinic. Many women and small children were waiting outside it. My mother went to talk to some of them, while I sat on the ground in the shade next to the container.

After a while she returned with a smile: 'The uncle isn't around, but he left a key for us with the neighbours. His place is near to the entrance.'

We walked back all the way we'd come, while the sun burned down on us. I felt dizzy, as I urgently needed something to drink. But our water bottle was empty and had been that way for a long time already. '*Hamba* – go, Mbu!' my mom told me. She did not pull me along, but was kinder than I was used to. She even comforted me, saying: 'We are almost there . . .'

Finally, we found the yard of this uncle and, luckily, one of the older neighbours was there and handed us the key: 'If you don't pay your rent, he will chase you away . . .' he said with a grumpy face. 'And if you make any trouble at night, we will all chase you out!' He then closed his door without another word.

But my mom seemed determined that life would become better here: 'Mbu, just wait until I have a job . . .' she told me.

As if to confirm her hopes she opened a tap next to the outside toilet. Clean water came out. '*Jonga* – you see!' I put my mouth under the tap and drank as much as I could. Maybe mom was right and things would be better in this place.

*

The shack was tiny and dark, even during the day, as it had no window, only a shrieking wooden door. There was no furniture and just a sandy floor. We were both so tired that mom unfolded a blanket on the ground and we lay down. We used her bag with all our clothes to put our heads on and fell asleep immediately.

The next morning my mom bought some apples, bananas and bread and we enjoyed our first breakfast in our new place. 'The rest of the money I must keep for the rent,' she told me.

She left me with one banana and a filled water bottle. '*Ndiyabuya ngoku* – I'm coming back soon, my boy!' she said. She went out, locking the wooden door from the outside. I was convinced that she would be back after an hour or so, as she had said many times how easy it was to get a job in *iKapa*. I imagined that we would buy some real groceries then, maybe even some sweets for me. And, one day, some furniture – a bed, and even a cupboard.

But mom did not come back soon, as I was expecting. Actually, she did not return the whole morning. The sun was high by now and the heat in the closed shack almost unbearable. It must have been around late morning when I felt the need to make a wee. First, I tried to ignore it but the need became stronger and stronger. I was convinced that my mother would become angry if I pee'd inside the shack. At the same time, I was afraid to call for help, since the old neighbour had been so unfriendly the day before.

Finally, I tried to open the door from the inside myself. But it was a strong lock, and although the door was wobbling, I could not make it open. Eventually I could not hold my wee in a second longer and pissed all over myself.

It was then that I started crying, although I had promised my mom that I would never cry in the new place. I felt so ashamed about myself. I was sweating and stinking and it was just so hot.

Maybe my mom had had an accident? Or somebody had robbed her of the rest of the money with which she had planned to pay the rent? I started to panic then, because I missed my older brother Mavusi so much.

Much later, I heard some heavy footsteps coming closer. 'Mom?' I asked in a low voice.

But then somebody started banging on the door: bang, bang, bang – three times.

I did not dare to make a sound. Who was banging so violently against the door?

'*Vula ucango* . . . open the door!' a male voice demanded. And again, more banging.

11

I put all my courage together and responded: '*Uxolo* – sorry, I can't. My mom is gone . . .'

I heard men talking to each other outside. Then they disappeared. And I kept waiting . . .

It was afternoon when my mom returned. She had no food with her.

She was so drunk that she did not even notice the bad smell in the shack. I ran out to the tap and drank and drank, as much as I could. Water helps when you are hungry. I knew that. But I also knew it never helps for long. The hunger always returns. Even worse.

That evening, I found something in a rubbish bin, close to our yard. I don't want to call it food. But I ate it. There are moments in life when you eat anything. Very bad moments.

*

Life in the new place was not much different from the old place. Each day my mom went out looking for work. I stayed behind with the other children in the yard. She no longer locked me into the shack, because we knew the neighbours now. The uncle who owned the yard was a nice man. I found out that he was my mother's brother. Sometimes he helped out with food. If it wasn't for that we would have starved.

Then, once again, there was hope in this new place.

It was about two weeks after our arrival when mom came home one day very excited: '*Enkosi Thixo* – thank God! I found a cleaning job not far from here . . . I can start tomorrow!'

The rest of that day she spent washing all our clothes with powder she had borrowed from the wife of the uncle. She hung everything carefully in the sun and watched over it to make sure nobody could steal anything.

The next evening, she brought home some fresh fruit and even a small piece of chicken. 'All from this kind family . . . They even promised us some furniture,' she told me.

And indeed, at the end of the week, an *umlungu*, a white man, brought mom home in a *bakkie* and unloaded a used mattress, two chairs and a camping table. 'Is this your son?' the man asked.

'*Ewe* – yes!' my mom answered. 'This is Mbu. He will go to school soon . . .'

I tried to look big, so that he would believe my mom. But I did not dare to say a word.

That evening, we sat on the two chairs and there was more food than ever before, set out on the small camping table. I asked my mom: 'Can I really go to school?'

'*Ndiya kuthembisa* – I promise!' she said.

And she really kept her promise. In fact, it was the only promise she ever made to me in her life. So, whatever you might think about my mom, at least she was always honest, despite all her other failings.

*

About one month later the happiest day of my life happened.

So far, I had not made real friends in Masiphumelele, partly because I still missed my brother so much. But there were a few girls in our yard who sometimes played *puca*, the popular stone-skipping game. As I was good at collecting the soft, round stones, they invited me from time to time to join them. It was on one such evening, when I was playing with the older girls, that my mom came down our road with a blue and white plastic bag from the local PEP store.

'*Yizapha* – come here, Mbu!' she called to me when she was

still a fair distance away on the road. I ran to her, as I could see the smile on her face. Had she really kept her promise?

She handed me the bag but did not allow me to open it. 'You must carry it home!' she said, and her order sounded like music in my ears.

I had my own key by now and unlocked our door impatiently. I put the bag down on the table and looked at her.

'*Vula ngoku* – open it now!' she told me.

My fingers were shaking from excitement and I almost tore the bag open. I could hardly believe my eyes at what I saw inside – a complete school uniform! All brand new. A yellow shirt with long sleeves, grey short pants and – above all – my first shoes ever: black and shiny!

'Can I really go to school?' I asked, my voice trembling.

'*Ngomso* – tomorrow you will start, my boy!' My mom's face wore a confident look, something I had never noticed before.

It was not only because of her joy for me; she was so proud of herself. This uniform was not donated, not second-hand stuff from other people. Nothing she had begged for. She had earned it with her own hands, paid for it with her own money.

She had gone to the store at the shopping mall by herself. She had looked for the right sizes and then queued for the cashier. How many people had seen her standing there? How many people had watched her opening her wallet and putting the whole amount on the table – more than One Hundred Rand! In cash. Nothing borrowed. Her own money. All by herself.

*

The next morning we got up very early as my mom wanted to accompany me to the school container before leaving for her work.

I was walking a bit funny as the new shoes were uncomfortable and chaffed against my feet, especially without socks. But the pain made me even more aware what a big day this was! I could go to Grade 1 in a new uniform – a luxury not even Mavusi had enjoyed.

The primary school in Masiphumelele at that time was not yet a brick building, just a few containers on an open field. But the people who had founded it had given it a most inspiring name: Ukhanyo School – *ukhanyo* meaning in isiXhosa *we bring the light!*

I felt I was the light that special morning, as I walked with my mom through the school gate and she guided me to the Grade 1 container. Inside it, an old lady was talking to a lot of small children. There were so many kids squeezed into that limited space that I could not even see any piece of the floor.

'*Wamkelekile* – welcome, Mbu!' the teacher said. And I knew I had made it.

It was such a lovely morning. I found a little space to sit down next to the other boys and girls on the floor, most of whom looked to be my age. I waved proudly to my mom so that she should know not to worry about me and go off to her work.

Later the teacher asked me: 'Mbu, can you sing?'

I answered: 'No, I can't . . . but I will learn. I want to learn so much!'

She gave me such a beautiful smile, that old teacher.

And I did learn to sing. Along with everyone else in assembly, I sang hymns, and found that I enjoyed singing.

I was right about schools: they can give you a special power. I was ready for any initiation . . .

3

Waiting at night
Ukulinda ebusuku

As far as I was concerned, this was the life I had always hoped for: my mom having a job and not drinking. Coming home to me in the evening without other men. Me going to school every morning, even if it was only Grade 1 so far and in an over-crowded container. I even enjoyed cleaning our shack in the afternoons.

And no more hunger, although we almost never ate chicken or fish, let alone real meat. Every day, we had what we called *African Salad*, which actually is not salad but *mealie meal* and sour milk. It is not tasty – it really has no taste at all – but the good thing about *African Salad* is: it can fill your tummy and you do not feel the pain of hunger.

I even began to like the ambitious name of this township, one of the poorest among the poor: Masiphumelele. In isiXhosa it means: 'We will make it'. And I thought, small as I was: I will make it, too!

But then everything changed, between one day and the next.

*

On that day I came home in a happy mood, as our teacher had told us that the whole class would soon go on an outing to the Zip Zap Circus in Cape Town, which was famous because all the performers in it were street kids. These kids were exceptionally good artists. They had performed on TV and even overseas. The nice rumour was that there were two girls from *Masi* who had made it to fame at the circus. Once or twice a year the circus invited primary classes from some of the townships – and this year Ukhanyo School had been chosen!

As I walked home, I thought about how I would share the good news with my mom that evening. I was sure she would be as happy for me as I was for myself.

When I turned into our yard, I could already see that something strange was happening. Our shack door was wide open. Had somebody tried to break into it?

I ran the rest of the way to our shack – and was shocked to see my mom sitting at the small table with her head bowed, holding her face in both hands. From the shivering of her back I could see that she was sobbing. I entered silently and put a hand on her shoulder: 'Mom?'

Only now did she notice me. When she turned her face towards me, I saw that tears were running all over her cheeks. She sighed deeply and said in a low voice: '*Kuphelile* – it's all over, Mbu! I got fired. They said that I stole something, but I did not . . .!'

Slowly I realised that my mother had lost her job, and that we would now have, from one day to the next, no money, no food, no nothing. I could not accept what I had just heard: '*Kodwa* . . . but, Mom, you will find another job! Please, don't give up now!'

I wasn't sure whether she had heard me. But finally she responded, in that same horrible, sad, low voice: '*Ubomi bunzima* – life is not good to me, Mbu!'

I wondered why she was talking only about herself and her

17

suffering. I wanted to say: but there is also me! Together we will make it! Don't give up now, mom! I am so good at school. You did so well working as a domestic with that family . . .

But it was as if nothing could make my mom return to the path of hope. As though she had read my thoughts, she continued: 'This is a small place here. They said they will tell everybody that I am dishonest – and that I will never find a job in this area again . . .!'

Sadly, I poured some sour milk for her and myself. She did not touch hers. She just sat there, until the evening dark came over us. I prepared our blankets for the night.

'*Lala kakuhle* – sleep well, Mom!' I tried to comfort her. 'Tomorrow is another day . . .'

But she was not ready to come to bed. She kept sitting where she was, on her chair, staring into a dark universe of her own. She did not respond to anything I said.

I covered myself with a blanket but I did not close my eyes. I was watching her, praying all the time: 'Please, God, give my mom another job tomorrow . . .!'

As she still did not relax and I got no sign from God, I started to negotiate: 'Please, God, give her a job next week. Or at least next month . . . please God!'

And, finally, I prayed: 'Even if she does not find any job at all, please, God, please, let her not start drinking again! Let her not go out again in the nights . . .'

*

When I left for school the following morning, mom was still asleep. Or so she pretended. I was relieved that she had stayed home at least, and assumed she had gone to bed much later, when I was already fast asleep.

I did not concentrate well at school that day. To be honest, I have no memory at all of what our teacher did with us in class that morning. On my way home, I was nervous and even ran the last few hundred metres. In what mood would I find my mom today?

But when I finally entered the shack, my mother was not there. I did not dare to ask any of the neighbours if they knew where she'd gone, and started to clean the house as always. By sunset, mom had still not returned home. My hope faded that she might have been out looking for another job.

Finally, it was pitch dark and there was still no sign of her. I went to bed, leaving the door open, in case she had lost her key. But I did not sleep; I was waiting for her.

She came at last, when the noise of all the other neighbours had already died down. So it must have been after midnight. I knew from her movements that I could make out in the moonlight, what had happened.

'Why are you not sleeping, *usana lwam* – my baby?' she asked in a high voice, holding herself upright against the door frame. She never called me 'baby' when she was sober.

A loud laugh came from her direction: 'All whites are shit . . .!' she said hoarsely. 'Black men are real men!'

I knew that in that state she would not listen to anything I had to say. She threw herself on the ground and started sobbing. I covered her with a blanket. I tried to sleep but I couldn't, not for a long time.

*

My wonderful old teacher noticed, as the days went by, how much I had changed.

'What is going on, Mbu? Every morning you look more tired! Are you not sleeping at all?'

I kept quiet, not wanting the other children to hear my troubles and make fun of me.

She didn't question me further. But she gave me, from time to time, a sandwich with jam on, as she could see how hungry I was. Even *African Salad* had run out in our shack.

But things got really bad when mom started to stay away all night with men again.

When I begged her to be with me at night, she responded angrily: '*Yima* – stop that, Mbu! Since we don't have money, I must try to find a decent man to take care of us. What else can I do?'

But she did not find either a job or a decent man, despite all her efforts.

One night she brought an older guy back to our place. Both of them were totally drunk and I tried my best to move myself away from them. But our shack was so small that their feet were touching me while they were having sex with each other. I am sure they did not even notice me there.

The following morning, I went to school as usual. But that was the first day that I could not hold my tears back when my teacher asked me again why I looked so tired . . .

*

That weekend, my mother confronted me with her final decision: 'This place is not good for you, Mbu. You must go back to *eRhafu*. I've found a guy to stay with here, but he has his own kids. I spoke to *Gogo* where Mavusi is staying, and she said you can also stay with her. You remember *Gogo*?'

Gogo – which means 'Granny' in isiXhosa – was not our real grandmother. She belonged to one of our family clans on my mother's side and was known for looking after children other than her own. She was a hard-working woman, with a reputation for being very strict with the kids. No one ever dared to object to anything she said.

I hadn't known that my beloved brother Mavusi was still with her. As much as I disliked the idea of leaving my mom behind and going to stay with *Gogo*, I was also excited by the thought of being reunited with Mavusi.

'Do you remember *Gogo*?' mom repeated impatiently.

'Yes, I do,' I replied. 'But who will pay for my bus ticket from here to there?'

'My new boyfriend will . . .' she said. But I could feel that she was not proud about it. It was just the way life was.

I was sad that I could not say goodbye to my kind old teacher since it was the weekend. I was also sorry to be missing the visit to the Zip Zap Circus that was scheduled for a few days later.

I had no luggage with me when my mom put me back on one of the same big buses that we had travelled on together to Cape Town a few months earlier. I'd left all my things behind in *Masi*, thinking I would be returning soon, when the holidays came. Mom took me to the bus station and made sure I got into the right coach. She did not wait with me until the bus left. And I did not cry.

I wondered whether Mavusi would be as happy to see me as I was at the thought of seeing him.

4

The best teacher ever
Oyena titshalakazi oqwesileyo

Nobody was waiting for me when I arrived the next morning, very early, at the taxi rank in Masizakhe. But I was old enough to find my way to *Gogo*'s home, which was a proper brick house, not a shack like many of the others.

It was Sunday and most people were still sleeping. The door of the green-painted brick house was locked.

I knocked once. Nothing happened. I knocked again, this time a bit more strongly. I heard somebody unlocking the door from the inside.

It was *Gogo*, still in her night gown, her glasses skew on her nose. She recognised me immediately: 'Are you here already? Your mother said on the phone you would only come tomorrow!'

I did not know what to answer. So I just asked: 'Is Mavusi here?'

Instead of answering my question, she asked: 'Don't you have any luggage? We don't have enough clothing for all the kids here as it is . . . and your mother promised to send you with stuff . . .'

Again I did not know what to say. Only now did I realise that my mother had even kept my school uniform, maybe for one of the kids of her new boyfriend to use. This made sense, as in Masizakhe school uniforms were different in colour from those in Masiphumelele.

Gogo did not seem to expect an answer from me. She waved me in and closed the door. She poured some milk in a cup and gave it to me. Then she commanded: 'Wash yourself . . . we are going to church in one hour. All of us!'

But I could not wait a moment longer to see Mavusi. When she returned to her bedroom, I went in search of my brother. Opening a door, I entered a room that had two beds in it. I could see several boys sleeping in each of the beds, and more on the floor. I whispered: 'Mavusi?'

Before I could get closer to the beds, I heard the loud voice of *Gogo* behind me: '*Vukani nonke* – get up all of you! In one hour we leave for church.'

I saw the boys crawling out of their beds; six boys altogether. And, finally, there he was!

'Mavusi!' I shouted, full of joy.

Mavusi was slower to recognise me. His response was much calmer than mine, but he at least had a smile: '*Molo, man* – hey, man,' he said, and gave me a hug.

It was so good to see him again. But how skinny he was! Even thinner than when we'd seen each other the last time.

'Are you sick, Mavusi?' I asked him.

'*Hayi, man* – no!' he answered. But a hard cough followed.

In no time all the children in *Gogo*'s house were ready for church.

Altogether we were seven boys and two girls, as well as an elderly sister of *Gogo*'s, and one of *Gogo*'s grown-up daughters. We were one of the first families to reach the church and were seated in the front row.

There was no chance to talk to Mavusi face to face. And the service seemed to be never ending. I glanced at him often as we sat there, and was disappointed that he hardly ever glanced back.

Finally, the service was over. I immediately ran to my brother. '*Uphila njani* – how is your life, Mavusi?'

'*Ndiphilile* – I am fine,' he said. But I saw that he was not.

And he did not ask me one question about how it had been with our mother far away in *iKapa*.

*

I realised with sadness that my dear brother, my hero, had changed during the past months. He had closed up and did not trust anybody anymore, not even me. He had found a group of older friends and was spending most of his spare time with them. He clearly did not want me hanging around with them. Mostly, they played soccer; some were smoking secretly.

Still, I never gave up hope that we would be brothers again like in the old days.

Though *Gogo* was strict with everybody and did not allow any nonsense, even from her own daughter, she did her best to send all of us to school. On the Monday morning after I'd arrived, she said to me: 'Don't think you can sleep longer than the others, Mbu! I can't buy you a uniform right now, but I know the principal of our primary school and I will ensure that you start there today.'

I felt a big smile grow on my face. I could continue to go to school!

'Don't smile at me!' *Gogo* said, with a serious face. 'If you are late getting to school or you don't do your homework, I will beat you. Got it?'

I stopped smiling; but inside, I was still so happy. I knew I would never be late or miss even a single day of school.

While *Gogo* was in the principal's office, talking behind closed doors, I looked around Masizakhe Primary School. It was a well-developed school with many prefab buildings, and even a gym and a soccer field.

A short time later, an older learner escorted me to one of the buildings close to the soccer field. 'Which grade are you?' he asked me.

I gathered all my courage together and said: 'Grade 1.'

He nodded and knocked at one of the classroom doors.

'*Ngena* – come in,' a soft female voice said from inside.

My escort opened the door, and I saw her for the first time – the best teacher ever in the whole world: Mrs Naki!

*

I am sure there must also be horrible teachers in this world. But Mrs Naki was an angel. She was about the same age as my mom, with beautiful eyes and full lips. Her cheeks were soft and when she spoke it sounded like gospel music. She wore her hair traditional style, braided with colourful beads.

I know it sounds funny coming from a seven-year-old boy, but it was love at first sight. Also from her side; I know that for sure. She never shouted at me. She took trouble to explain to me what I had missed in the first few months of Grade One, and she never called me stupid as *Gogo* did so many times.

I learnt to deal with *Gogo* because of Mrs Naki. Whenever I felt hurt by *Gogo*'s remarks or when she gave us a beating with her walking stick, I thought of Mrs Naki. I thought: you cannot break me, because I have her. You cannot make me stupid, because I learn everything from her.

Mrs Naki saw that many kids came hungry to school in Masizakhe. So she made us bread rolls, with small pieces of meat inside. We called them Hamburgers!

Some of the kids had parents with jobs. They had to buy the Hamburgers for R2 each. I volunteered to sell them during the long break. There was already a group of other learners doing this, but I became one of the best at it. One break time, I sold 57 Hamburgers in fifteen minutes – the school record was 51!

That day Mrs Naki asked me if I would like to come to her house for a home visit. I could not believe my luck. This was the way to heaven! But I was sure that *Gogo* would never allow it. As on so many other occasions, Mrs Naki seemed able to read my concerns.

'Shall I phone your *Gogo* for permission?'

I nodded my head, and began to pray for a good outcome immediately. And the miracle happened.

'She said it's okay,' Mrs Naki confirmed with a smile. 'As long as you are home not later than six.'

*

From that day on, I visited Mrs Naki at least three afternoons every week. I'd been so curious to know what her family would be like, since she never mentioned anything in class: did she have children? A husband? Would the other kids be jealous of me going home with her? Would her husband?

It turned out that Mrs Naki had no children and no husband – at least, not staying with her. She lived in a modest but lovely little brick house, with her younger brother and sister. And both of them were just as nice to me as she was.

The younger brother, Ayanda, had finished high school but could not find any work. 'We are saving up money for his studies,' Mrs Naki explained. 'One day he will be an engineer!' The sister, Andiswa, nodded her head: 'And me, too!'

Some afternoons, I walked with Ayanda to deliver his job application letters to all kinds of shops and little businesses in Graaff Reinet. 'I can't just sit and wait and let my sister do all the work,' Ayanda said. 'And, besides, I need a job – it doesn't matter what it is – so I can save money for my studies later . . .'

'Don't you have parents?' I asked him while we were walking home one afternoon from Graaff Reinet.

'No,' Ayanda said. He was silent for a long time. I did not press him, knowing that I had to wait.

We were already at the entrance to Masizakhe when he stopped walking and took hold of my hands: 'Our father and mother both died many years ago because of Aids. I was just your age, and our oldest sister was only thirteen . . . she's been looking after us ever since, while we finished our schooling.'

'You are such a good family,' I said deeply moved, thinking of my own broken one. I still had a mother but far away in *iKapa*, and a father somewhere in South Africa. And a brother who was like a stranger to me since my return.

Ayanda saw the tears that came up in my eyes. 'You won't cry, Mbu, will you?'

'No, I will not,' I said with determination.

*

I kept going to Mrs Naki's home to be with her and her family whenever I could. I still called her Mrs Naki (though I knew by then that her first name was Asethu), but I called her brother Ayanda and her sister Andiswa by their first names.

Everybody had special tasks in the family. I was good at cleaning the floors with a mop and soapy water. And I was the best at polishing their red stoep. I did it all alone and was so happy when Mrs Naki said: 'Looks like it's freshly painted, Mbu!'

I slept at *Gogo*'s house and I had breakfast there with the other kids. But after school I'd go to Mrs Naki's. Only on the weekends did *Gogo* not allow me to join the Naki family.

'As long as you stay in my house you'll go to church with us, Mbu,' she had told me once. I did not dare to ask again.

Even worse than weekends were the Christmas holidays. All the foster kids were allowed to travel to their relatives; it was only Mavusi and I who had to stay behind. We had to do the chores of all the others, like helping with cooking or dishwashing, cleaning the yard or fetching water. And there was no escape from yet more church services.

'I want to go and see how our mother is, Mavusi,' I said to my brother one evening, as we each lay alone in a big, empty bed all to ourselves.

'I don't,' said Mavusi, and turned his back to me.

His health was no better than when I'd first arrived. He had to take pills that the doctors at the hospital had given him for his coughing, but they did not seem to help much.

In my second year at *Gogo*'s, our mom phoned at Christmas. I was allowed to speak to her.

'When can we come and visit you, Mom?' I asked.

'*Unyako olandelayo* – next year, my baby!' she said, and I knew that she was not sober.

The following year at Christmas when she phoned, she said the same thing.

Mavusi refused to talk to her at all.

*

Time went on and without my regular visits to Mrs Naki and her siblings my life at *Gogo*'s would have been much more difficult. I felt that I had another family when I was with them.

By then, I was eleven already. One day I made a bad mistake: I lied to *Gogo*. She always told us that she would never forgive two things: stealing and lying.

But I was just so tired of going to church. So one Sunday morning, I told *Gogo*: '*Mamela* – listen, Mrs Naki has asked me to come to her house as her sister is very sick and she needs extra help.'

'*Intoni* – what? Can you tell me what disease she has?' *Gogo* asked suspiciously.

'She has a high fever,' I kept lying.

Fortunately, *Gogo* did not phone Mrs Naki to check on the story.

When I arrived at my teacher's little brick house, she looked surprised but glad to see me: 'How nice to see you on a Sunday, Mbu. Did your *Gogo* allow you to come?'

'Yes,' I lied again. The rest of that Sunday was just wonderful, as always when I was there. Mrs Naki, Ayanda and Andiswa prayed before meals but never went to church.

The following weekend I invented a new and more creative story and told *Gogo* that a water pipe had broken in Mrs Naki's house and that she'd asked if I could come and help her brother with digging the trenches to the water connection in the garden.

Surprisingly, *Gogo* just looked at me and said: '*Hamba* – go, Mbu!'

I was already at the gate when I heard her calling my name. Hesitantly I walked back into the living room.

Gogo grabbed me by my left ear and pulled me up with it until it was really painful. Then she shouted into it: 'I know that you are a liar, boy! I just want you to know that I don't take liars with me to church ...'

She let me go without further comment. I was surprised at how easily I'd got off. The other kids went to church as usual but I stayed home.

When I told Mavusi later what happened, he just looked at me. Then he said: 'Mbu, do you always think you are special?'

'No,' I responded, 'but *Gogo* is not like a mother to us ... she is like a general.'

I could see that he did not want to talk to me. It made me so sad.

*

And another year passed. I'd turned twelve now, but my birthday was never celebrated. Still, I accepted life as it was.

I was very grateful to be with Mrs Naki and her siblings as often as I was. But I also understood that I could not stay with them permanently, since Mrs Naki was my teacher and many other kids in the class would have wanted the same. As it was, I was already so privileged with my visits.

It was in January 2005 that my life took an unexpected turn again. Most of the other kids had gone to their relatives as usual and Mavusi and I had just received another phone call from our mother.

I had told a neighbour of ours, a young woman called Zoleka, that I had not seen my mother for five years and that I would like to visit her, even if only once. I said it without expecting anything. But Zoleka mentioned it to *Gogo*, and the two women started shouting at each other.

'Why do you never allow Mbu to see his mother? That is cruel!' Zoleka fired at *Gogo*.

Gogo hit back: 'Who do you think you are, Zoleka? What do you know? Do you take care of any children at all? Mbu's mother does not care about him. She sends no money. Must I even pay for the ticket, then?'

'You never say anything nice about Mbu!' Zoleka shouted back. 'Why don't you let him decide if he wants to see her? He's not a baby anymore!'

Suddenly *Gogo* looked at me: 'Do you want to go to your mother, Mbu?'

I nodded my head. A second later, *Gogo* grabbed me by the arm and pushed me back into the house: '*Ngoku* – now, Mbu, put your stuff together and go! I will take you to the bus station right now!'

Zoleka shut her mouth in surprise. Mavusi shook his head like he thought I was just crazy. Then he walked back into his room.

I wanted to say goodbye to Mrs Naki, Ayanda and Andiswa, at least, but *Gogo* didn't let me go anywhere. 'I will tell Mrs Naki tomorrow. She had enough time with you these past years.'

She then pushed me out of the house and together we marched straight to the bus station. There she negotiated with one of the drivers, all the while watching me closely to make sure I didn't run off anywhere.

We had to wait about an hour until departure. Neither of us said a word in all that time.

I climbed onto the bus with the other passengers. This time I had luggage, a small suitcase that Mavusi had given me along with some of his clothes. *Gogo* was still watching me, but she did not wave as the bus started to move.

The driver shouted to me so that all the other passengers heard: 'Your mother must pay for the trip; just so that you know, boy!'

I looked down and did not say a word. How would mother receive me after all these years?

5

My friends Yamkela and Atie
Abahlobo bam uYamkela noAtie

When the minibus taxi turned into the entrance road to Masiphumelele everything still looked familiar, although it was five years since I had left. Some changes had come in my absence: there were more tarred roads and brick houses and most of the streets now had names and lights.

'Where is your mother to pay for your ticket?' the driver asked in a grumpy tone once all the other passengers had got off. I had no idea, not even a clue where she now stayed. But *Gogo* had given me a small piece of paper with a cell number written on it. 'That's the number of her new boyfriend or husband or whatever . . .' she'd said.

I asked the driver to phone the number and he did so. 'She is on her way,' he told me, obviously tired from driving through the night.

And suddenly there she was. She looked so much older and smaller than in my memory. Or was it only because I had grown a lot?

'*Goh* – what a tall boy you are, Mbu!' she said, and gave me a cautious hug. Despite the long time that had passed since our last contact and all her neglect over the years, I was just so happy to see her. After all, she was my mom. I thought about Mrs Naki and her siblings Ayanda and Andiswa; at least I still had a mom.

'*Molo, Mama* – hello, Mom!' I responded and kissed her on her cheek.

I was nervous about whether she could pay the driver. But she pulled some notes from her pocket and handed the money over.

'*Enkos' buthi* – thank you for bringing my son home.'

I could not wait to see my mother's house. Judging from her neat appearance and clean dress she was not as desperate as she had been the last time I'd seen her.

'I have a permanent job now,' she told me confidently. 'I do shift work in a factory, packing milk boxes.'

We walked to her house along the main road and turned into a yard with a brick house in the front and several small shacks behind it. The house was freshly painted; we passed it and walked to one of the poorer-looking shacks right at the back. I heard a small child crying inside. For a moment it was like a flashback in time – and I felt as if I was the baby left alone in the shack.

'That's Anam, your little half sister. She just turned one,' my mother told me. She unlocked the old door and we entered the small shack, made of cardboard and wood with a plastic-sheeting roof, like most of the other shacks.

It was dark inside and the first thing I noticed was the smell of dirty nappies from the baby. Then my eyes got a bit more used to the gloom and I saw that most of the tiny shack was occupied by a large bed and a small cupboard next to it. The floor was covered with an old grey carpet which had lost its colour.

'It's so good for Anam that you are here,' my mom said; and, indeed, Anam did not cry anymore, but gave me a cute smile.

'Do you see her first two teeth?' mom pointed out proudly. Anam started giggling, exposing her two new top front teeth beautifully.

'I've bought some bread and polony for you, Mbu,' my mom said, handing me a plastic bag. 'Please give Anam her bottle of milk powder mixed with water in an hour or so . . .'

Before I could ask any questions she put on blue overalls and handed me a key: 'I will be back in the early evening. You might meet the father of Anam before my return as he is on day shift today . . .'

She went out. And there I was alone with a little baby girl next to me, my so-called half sister. I first went out to the water tap and then to the only toilet, shared by all those who were living in the backyard; I had counted five shacks. I used the toilet and afterwards washed myself under the tap, Anam sitting on the ground, observing my movements.

I made her a bottle of milk and she drank it happily, although it was not even warmed up. I was too tired to explore further and, locking the door from the inside, threw myself on the bed with all my clothes on. Anam crawled around next to me for a while on the big bed and finally cuddled against my tummy.

We both feel asleep soon after that.

*

My flashback in time was not over yet. I had horrible dreams of violent people shouting and banging with sticks against the walls of the room I was locked in. They shouted: '*Siyakubetha* – we beat you . . . we get you . . .'

I tried to run away but strong ropes were around my arms and legs and I was naked like a baby, although the same boy of twelve as in real life. I was tall and strong, but I was crying for help and my cries had a hundred echoes . . . sweat ran all over my body . . . a total panic had hold of me. *Ndincede . . . ndinceeeede* – help . . . heeelp . . .!

I woke up. Indeed, I was sweating all over and next to me, Anam was crying. Just as in my dream I was in a dark room and somebody was banging against the door. '*Vula ngoku* – open now!' a male voice was shouting angrily.

I jumped up from the bed and hastily opened the door: 'Uxolo – sorry!' I mumbled, trying to make out who the man was. Was this the father of Anam?

'Hayi – never lock the door from the inside again!' he said, without even greeting me. 'This is my house and I am the only one who locks it from the inside!'

Then he looked at me curiously: 'You must be Mbu?'

I nodded shyly. 'And you are the father of Anam?'

'I am your mother's husband,' was his answer. 'My name is Siya.' We shook hands like men.

He looked like he was in his late thirties or early forties. I was wondering why he and my mother still lived in such poor conditions when they both had jobs. But I did not dare to ask.

Opening the door of the cupboard, Anam's father took out bread and other things and made himself a sandwich. I also saw some beer bottles next to the bread. He did not offer me anything. And I did not ask. I thought I had better wait for my mother to come back.

As there was so little space in the shack he sat on the bed while he ate. Anam received another bottle, this time from her father, who had warmed it on a small paraffin stove. I sat outside and waited for my mother to return.

It was dark when she finally arrived from work. She had two bottles of fresh milk and a tin of soup with her.

We ate the heated soup soon afterwards and my mom and Siya each drank one of the bottles of beer. When he opened a second and then a third bottle, my mom said in a low voice: 'Not tonight, please! It's his first night . . .'

The man who called himself my mother's husband looked irritated; but he put the fourth bottle back in the cupboard.

My mother then prepared their bed for the night. I was wondering where I was supposed to sleep. My mom looked at Siya, but he just shook his head. She put one of the blankets down on the old carpet.

'You will sleep on the floor, Mbu . . . if you get cold we can give you another blanket.'

I should not have gone to sleep during the day, since I was much too wide awake now. First the baby fell asleep; shortly afterwards, I could hear the deep snoring of the man and then my mother's lighter snores. I lay listening to the sounds from outside; so many sounds . . . barking dogs . . . shouting people in a *shebeen* somewhere . . . the hooting of cars far away. I just couldn't fall asleep. I also did not want to dream again.

The carpet had a bad smell and was wet close to the wall.

*

I counted the days until school would start. I was in Grade 5 now and, thanks to Mrs Naki, I was not afraid of any subjects in class. Aside from the factory job, my mom was also doing the washing for some neighbours in exchange for small amounts of money or food. Just before the holidays ended, she brought home a used school uniform that was almost my size.

'In a few months it will fit you perfectly,' she said. I was grateful indeed that she had received the uniform, just in time, through one of her laundry jobs.

I'd been back at home for almost two weeks now and I'd started to accept that my mother and this man were drinking every evening. They did not go to bed without being totally drunk. Sometimes they were joined by neighbours who also drank and made a lot of noise. If they had no booze left in the cupboard, they went to other people or to one of the *shebeens*.

I felt sure that this man had accepted my return only because I looked after Anam whenever I could. I was normally the one who put her to bed and made her last bottle of the day. Anam was incredibly sweet . . . she had a smile like a star in the night. I could not understand why she was always smiling, whereas I had always been crying as a baby . . .

*

On my first day back at Ukhanyo Primary School I was impressed to find that it was now a beautiful brick building, painted in bright yellow, with real classrooms and a huge roofed courtyard in the centre of it. The principal, Mr Thyali, always wore a perfectly ironed shirt with a tie, and the week started with school assembly for all the learners, with a prayer and announcements by the principal. Hundreds of learners stood together, listening to Mr Thyali, or bowing their heads for the prayer.

After that we marched to our classrooms. My teacher was Mr Honono who was one of the older teachers. There were about fifty learners in the class and everybody respected Mr Honono. Of course, I missed Mrs Naki, but I know that this teacher also did his best for us. He taught us EMS, which stood for Economics, Measurements and Science. In Economics he would talk to us about saving money and avoiding debts. 'Only buy with the money you have,' he'd say. 'Everything else means trouble!'

In Life Orientation he spoke about eating healthy food. 'Don't eat junk food like white bread. Always brown bread!' Then he'd unwrap his daily sandwich and, yes – it was brown bread!

On occasion, when he was tired and some of us were too rowdy in class, he would command the culprits to the front and give us a beating with a plastic pipe on our fingers. No one questioned that he had the right to do so. Most of the kids there were also beaten at home.

It was here at Ukhanyo that I started enjoying soccer. I had never played it with my brother Mavusi in Masizakhe. But here I did. In time, I became a really good midfielder. I had long legs and could run fast. But the best thing about soccer was my first friend, Yamkela. He played in the same team as I did. There was never any competition between us. He'd pass to me whenever he could and I did the same for him. Many times he shared his sandwich with me at break time, as I never had any food to take to school.

Since we were friends we also spent time together in the afternoons after school. It never bothered him that I had Anam with me. He knew that my mother and Anam's father got drunk every evening.

One night, Siya handed me a bottle, still half full of beer. 'You want to be a man one day? Then you must learn to drink early . . .'

My mom did not say anything. I took the bottle and drank it down with one gulp. The beer came from the *shebeen* and was still *lekker* cold. I was about fourteen by then.

*

From that evening, I started drinking myself. Mostly, when my mom and this man were already asleep, I would finish off any beer that remained in the bottles. I discovered that beer was also good against hunger.

Unfortunately, there was not only a lot of drinking going on in our yard. Some of the guys, and also some of the women, became quite ugly when they were drunk. They started arguing and fighting about everything – money, food, drinks and, sometimes, about the 'ladies'.

One evening, Siya accused another man in our yard of touching my mom while Siya was on shift. The man responded aggressively: 'Your wife is a whore . . . she shows her fat breasts to everybody. You must teach her a lesson, not me . . .'

My friends Yamkela and Atie

My mom started crying and Siya took a bottle and hit it against the neighbour's head without any warning. It was a full bottle, heavy with beer and it knocked the man out immediately. Strangely, nobody seemed to care about the bleeding man lying on the ground. 'His head is made of stone,' laughed Siya, and most of the others joined in his laughter.

That evening was the first that I went walking. I checked briefly on Anam and when I saw her sleeping despite all the commotion, I left the yard and walked down the main road. To begin with I had no aim; I just walked and walked until the road ended, vanishing into the wetland area where there are still many shacks but no more street lights. I turned around and walked back the way I'd come, then started to walk in circles, walking and walking; I just did not want to return to that place of shouting and drinking.

It was only when somebody called my name that I realised which road I was in.

'Mbu?'

It was Yamkela calling my name. He stood in front of the little brick house in which he lived with his mother. I was ashamed that he should see me like that; it was obvious to everyone that I had also drunk beer, just from the smell.

'*Ngena* – come in, Mbu!' Yamkela said, and closed the door behind me. Without another word he opened the fridge and gave me some leftovers from their supper – a piece of real chicken, and potato salad. What a taste! I licked each of my fingers.

'*Enkos*' – thank you, Yamkela!' I said. I looked around for his mother. 'Is she sleeping?'

'No,' he told me. 'She's working night shift at the old age home in Fish Hoek . . . three or four nights a week.'

I felt that I should not abuse any more of his kindness. I stood up and thanked him again.

When I was at the door already, he asked: 'Why don't you sleep here tonight?'

What a generous offer. 'But your mom, Yamkela?'

'She knows you are my friend,' he said, and locked the door twice from the inside.

*

From then on I stayed over at least two nights a week at Yamkela's place. His mother always welcomed me and once even said: 'I am happy you're here, because I know my son is not alone when I'm on night shift.' They always had such lovely food and most times kept something for me.

They even had a TV and we were allowed to watch whatever we liked. No age restriction. Funnily enough, we both did not like the crime movies, with all their violence of beatings and shootings and murder. But we did like the so-called 'adult' movies . . . beautiful girls and women making love with men, and all the stories around that. That's what we liked the most. But we did not tell anyone else what we watched.

When I came home the next morning, after my first night at Yamkela's, neither my mom nor Siya asked where I had been. It seemed as if they were satisfied when I told them that I had been with a friend. Maybe they'd just enjoyed having a little bit more space in the shack.

This pattern went on for more than a year, until I met my second best friend – Atie. Atie was two years younger than me, but he was a strong guy and looked older than his age. I had heard about him even before I met him in person: Atie – the one with the big mouth!

Atie was what you could call a survivor. He knew how to look after himself. Where I was sad, Atie laughed. Where I was angry and kept quiet, Atie shouted back. Where I would run away, Atie would attack, no matter how strong the opponent was.

What I did not know at the time was that once Atie had chosen you as his friend, he would never, never, never let you down. He was just so loyal. And he knew how to enjoy life.

'*Yonwabele* – enjoy!' he would say, when we had spent a whole afternoon collecting metal from rubbish bins, or asking neighbours for permission to dismantle their old fridges or washing machines. We then took it all to a scrapyard, where we received a few coins for two heavy bucket-loads of good metal: R5, sometimes R8 or R10.

'Enjoy!' Atie said, and we would buy one Coke, or an ice cream, or one bag of chips, and share it. We shared everything.

Around this time my mom became pregnant again. She lost her job in the factory and stayed home, because she was not feeling well most of the time. I was sitting in the yard one evening with Anam and my mom when Atie came by to pick me up for what we called a 'walk'. A walk means to go looking for adventure, for fun, for excitement, small as it may be; or just to hang out together, sharing the latest jokes.

On that particular evening one of the neighbours was already quite drunk, though it was still early and Siya wasn't home yet. Most of the other people in the yard had just come home from work. This drunk guy was talking rudely to my mom, asking her whether she was sure that Siya really was the father of her unborn child. Atie saw how hurt my mom was, and while I kept silent, Atie shouted back: 'Hey, brush your stinking mouth before you talk to a lady!'

Everybody in the yard burst out laughing. There was this big, drunk, rude man standing there with his mouth hanging open, not knowing what to say to this small, fearless boy.

'Ready for a walk?' Atie asked me.

Yes, I was ready. I did not know at the time that one day there would be a last walk for Atie.

6

Father: Where are you?
Tata: Uphi?

Like me, Atie did have parents. I don't know where his mother was, and I am not sure whether even Atie knew. But he had a father who stayed in a shack in Masonwabe Road with his stepmother and his much younger half brother, Malibongwe. Sometimes his father disappeared to Capricorn, a mixed township of black and coloured people near to Vrygrond. It's possible that he also had family there.

Families, families, families. I really don't know what a family is. Some people say: it is a father, a mother and children. But I hardly know any families like that. I know adults who have split up with their partners and have half families here and half families there – and maybe a quarter family somewhere else. Usually, when a man meets a woman or a woman meets a man, they start with having sex with each other, and, sometimes, they call it love.

Some of them move in together for a while and pretend to be happy. You don't have to wait long for the day they start arguing. The next step is: they shout. Then they fight. They throw things at each other. Sometimes the men beat the women. Sometimes the women cheat with other men. When men have sex with other women, it's not called cheating. When men make babies with other women, they mostly don't care. They don't care about the babies or the women or themselves – not even about Aids. That's why you see so many mothers with kids without fathers. Does any of this make sense?

The best family I ever met was one that you might call a 'child-headed household': Mrs Naki and her two siblings. The second best is a small Children's Home with kind childcare workers, most of them young adults and all from Masiphumelele, who look after kids that don't have anyone to take care of them. But about this place, I will tell you more later.

At the time that I'm speaking about, Atie and I honestly did not know what a family is. Neither of us wanted to marry and have kids, although, of course, there was the challenge that there were some quite attractive girls around. But how to be friends with them? No idea. Maybe sex, yes, when we were a bit older; soon.

But this thing called love, or even having our own family in the future? No idea. One day Atie said: 'Wouldn't you like to know how white *chicks* are in bed? Maybe it's easier with them.'

That's the language Atie used; sorry. And, of course, he was always ready to venture into new territory. He loved challenges.

For now, it wasn't a problem for him that his father and stepmother had just split up again after a period of fighting with each other, and that Atie's dad was staying in Vrygrond most of the time. Atie was used to fending for himself.

Next to their shack, there was a small, empty caravan. 'This will be our shack, when my dad is not around,' Atie suggested one evening. We started to fix up the caravan, plugging the holes in the roof with plastic bags. We then collected all kinds of stuff from the rubbish dump to put in it.

But don't think we had an ugly, stinking place; this caravan became one of the best! Before we brought anything in, we washed and scrubbed it with soap and dried it in the sun. In the end, we had almost everything we needed – a small mattress, a cupboard, even a table.

On top of all that, Atie managed to connect an illegal wire to another illegal wire – and from that day on we even had electricity! That meant: light, music, an old computer, even a small black and white TV. The caravan in Masonwabe Road was a hundred times better than the shack of my mother.

I moved away from them permanently, though I missed Anam. Fortunately, by then our Auntie Nompumelelo had also moved into her own shack in our yard and looked after the small ones when my mom and Anam's father were not around. But I kept worrying about my newborn half brother Aphelele. He was such a tiny little guy, always crying, like me when I was a baby.

*

It was around this time that Atie asked me one evening: 'What happened to your *tata*? I mean the real one, your blood father.'

'Good question,' I answered.

The last time I had seen my father I was still a toddler. Mom almost never mentioned him to me, and certainly not in the presence of Siya.

What kind of man was he? Why had he left? Maybe it was all my mother's fault, with her drinking. Did he also drink? Maybe he just had enough and went to start a nice family somewhere else. But why did he never try to find out about Mavusi or me? I knew that Mavusi also had no clue about our father's whereabouts.

Somehow, Atie's question had triggered a lot of fantasies. Most of them were actually good ones: imagine if my father also thought about me sometimes. Maybe he was even missing his son – me – just a little bit. Imagine if he had also been clever at school like me, and had a good job somewhere. He might even live in a proper house . . . he might be hoping that I would find him one day.

Another week passed before I found the chance to ask my mother about my real father without Siya around.

She grew upset immediately: '*Haybo* . . . why are you asking me about him? He never paid anything towards his children, so how would I have your father's details?'

'But why did he leave us all those years ago and never come back?' I persisted.

'How do I know? He just left . . . he never told me why.'

And then I made her really upset: 'Was it because you were drinking too much?'

She put her hands on her hips and shouted so that all the neighbours could hear: 'Who are you to talk to me like that? Did I not always look after you?'

When I did not respond, she added: 'Go and find your wonderful father yourself!' And slammed the door.

I thought: yes, that's exactly what I must do. But how?

*

As I walked slowly out of the yard, I saw Auntie Nompumelelo peeping out of her doorway, gesturing silently for me to come closer. Auntie Nompumelelo was, in fact, the sister of my mother, a real blood aunt.

'Mbu,' she said in a low voice, once I was inside her shack, 'I have lost track of your father, but I remember that he started a new family some years ago in Gugulethu. One of his sisters also lives in the area. I myself haven't seen him for years. But I still have his address in *Gugs*; it's a road called NY 112. Do you want to give it a try?'

Gugulethu, or *Gugs* as it is called, is one of the biggest

45

townships around Cape Town, with a few hundred thousand residents. It would not be easy to track my father down in such a place. But Auntie Nompumelelo knew the name of the road at least, although she couldn't remember the house number. That would certainly help.

My aunt had another surprise for me: 'You know what, Mbu? I was hoping that you would one day ask about your father. I've saved some money for this exact occasion . . .'

She went to a locked cupboard and opened one of the drawers.

'Here, Mbu . . .' she said, handing me a R50 note. 'This should be enough to catch a minibus taxi to *Gugs*. Ask the driver how to get to NY 112 . . .'

'*Enkos' kakhulu, Makazi* – thank you so much . . . I will find him, I promise you!'

I needed a few days to prepare for my trip and also to wait for the weekend, since I didn't want to miss school. Every evening, I ended my prayers by asking God to let me find my father. I felt so confident somehow that I would find him . . . and that he would be happy to see me again. He would be proud of me. And maybe I would even stay with him. Maybe my life would change forever.

Three days later, the Easter holidays began. I left on the first day, early in the morning, without telling anybody. Only my aunt knew; nobody else. Not even Yamkela or Atie.

*

The first part of my journey was no problem. When the minibus taxi drew up at the big taxi ranks in *Gugs*, I asked the driver if he could tell me where NY 112 was. He said: '*Lula* – that's easy! Just follow this road to the next traffic lights. Then turn to the right and walk another ten minutes. NY 112 is on your left-hand side . . .'

I was carrying only a small bag but had taken all the important stuff with me. Even my latest school report and my toothbrush.

A short walk later, I spotted the NY 112. Close to the corner, there was a *spaza* shop selling loaves of bread, cigarettes, sweets, cold drinks and other things. I went in and asked the old lady behind the counter whether she knew Mr Maloni.

'*Ngubani igama* – what's the name?'

I repeated my father's surname. But she had no idea who he was. '*Andimazi* – I don't know him . . .' she said.

Maybe she was new to the area? I walked on further down the road, stopping people at random: 'Mr Maloni? Do you know him? He's my father.'

I started to get really despondent when I reached the end of NY 112 and still nobody had given me the answer I needed to my question. Had he perhaps died? Had he moved somewhere else? Please, God, please . . .

I was on the point of giving up when one of the elderly neighbours of the *spaza* shop waved to me to come back to him: 'Did you say Maloni? Funny name! Yes, there was a guy living here. But he moved from here long ago. His sister is still around, though. Do you see the shack on the other side of the road? The greenish one? That's where she still stays with his kids . . .'

His kids? So he had another family here? But why had he moved on again?

Nervously I crossed the road. The door was open and I saw a boy and girl of about ten and twelve years old watching TV inside. At the back of the house a woman was hanging her washing.

I greeted her and asked: 'Do you know the Maloni family?'

Drying her hands on her skirt, she came towards me.

'Yes,' she said, looking surprised. 'I am Mr Maloni's sister and he is the father of these children. Who are you?'

'I am his son, his second born.'

She looked at me in amazement for a second. 'I can see that you are my brother's son,' she said.

She invited me to come in.

In the house I was introduced to the boy, called Andile, and the younger girl, called Noma. 'This is Mbu, your half brother,' she said to the children.

Andile made some space for me on the sofa: 'Do you want to watch *Generations* with us?'

I sat down, but I could not focus on the soapy. I was too busy asking the woman questions about my father: 'Why does he not stay with his children? Where is he now?' And, finally: 'Did he ever mention me?'

The woman, my new auntie, gave me honest answers: 'He was fighting too much with his girlfriend, the mother of these two, you know. When he got an RDP house in Blikkiesdorp recently he moved there alone and left the kids with me. At least he sends money sometimes, when he has a job . . . but you know, it's the old trouble. He is just drinking too much.'

'And did he ever say anything about me or my brother Mavusi?'

'No, not really. He only mentioned once that he has children somewhere in the Eastern Cape . . .'

After everything she'd told me, I didn't know what to do. I sat watching TV with Andile for hours without seeing anything of what was on the screen. Andile had switched to a soccer game, but I did not even notice who was playing. I felt like I was paralysed. I could not even pray anymore.

When it grew dark, Andile's aunt said to me: 'Why don't you stay with us tonight? Andile will be going to pick up some things from his father tomorrow and he can show you where he stays in Blikkiesdorp . . .'

Blikkiesdorp was an Afrikaans name for the new settlement in Delft where the government had erected more than a thousand matchbox houses for poor people. A *blik* is a tin can . . . and that is how most of the houses looked. All alike, hundreds and hundreds of them.

I did not sleep much that night. I heard the snoring of my auntie and her two children. I thought about my coming visit to my father's new place in the morning, and was glad that Andile was going with me. I knew that I would never find this man, my father, in Blikkiesdorp without him.

We left early the next day. Andile's kind auntie gave both of us money for the minibus taxi.

*

It's hard to know what to say about my meeting with the man who is my father. It didn't take us long to get to Blikkiesdorp, since it's not far from *Gugs*. When we arrived, Andile walked confidently ahead, finding his way through the tin cans without difficulty. They all looked the same to me, but he seemed to know where he was going. He knocked at the door of one of the *blikkie* houses; a man opened and gave the boy a hug. He looked at me and I knew that he did not recognise me. I didn't recognise him, either.

I said: 'It's me. Mbu.'

He still did not remember me. Not even my name.

I said again: 'Mbu, your son.'

He gave a shy smile: '*Uxolo* – sorry, boy. Yes, yes, now I see. Come in!'

He did not hug me. He asked me about my school, but I did not show him my good report.

He shared a sandwich and a Coke with Andile and me. Then he gave Andile a bag with clothes and some cash. A short while later, Andile left to go back to *Gugs*.

I asked my father if I could stay for a while. In the end, I remained with him for almost two weeks. In that time, he did not answer one of my questions honestly. He just said 'Yes' or 'No' or 'I don't know'. He did not ask about Mavusi, not once. Nor about his sister in *Gugs*.

In the evenings he drank as much as mom did.

After two weeks, I asked him for transport money back to Masiphumelele. He gave me R40, two notes of twenty.

The morning I left my father, I realised that I had done no prayers for two weeks.

I told Auntie Nompumelelo that her brother had moved to Delft. I also gave her the street name and number of his new place. My mom did not ask where I had been for the past two weeks. And I did not tell her.

Atie, I told: 'I found my father . . .'

'And?' Atie asked.

'*Okukho nto* – nothing,' I said.

7

Growing up wild
Ukukhula ngaphandle kwe-nkathalelo

With that caravan, Atie and I finally had our own roof over our heads – this was just great. But how to get food, clothing, stationery and books for school, all that stuff? From time to time, Atie received pocket money from his dad, which he generously shared with me. And from time to time I still got delicious leftovers from Yamkela's mom or from my Auntie Nompumelelo, which Atie and I also shared. I was just worried about my school uniform, which fell apart more and more. And there were many evenings when we went to bed hungry . . .

One evening, Atie came with a new idea: '*Mamela* – listen, Mbu! We can earn some good money with the *tik* guys!'

I'd been afraid that he would one day come with some such nonsense. Everybody knew that the drug lords recruited young ones like us to sell *tik*, to get us into using the hard stuff.

'*Hayi* – no, Atie! That's a bad idea, just bad. The police are watching them all the time: one day you are rich, the next day you are in Pollsmoor prison.'

I was prepared to have to argue with Atie about it. But to my surprise, he responded: '*Ndiyavuma* – I agree. That stuff is actually pure shit . . .'

Still, we had to get what we needed from somewhere. Somehow. The scrapyard thing was for kids. We needed something better.

Soon I would start going to Masiphumelele High School. Despite all my troubles, my latest report from Grade 7 at primary school was one of the best. I had not missed one single school day in the last term.

I was sure that the new principal at our high school, Mr Mafrika, would not tolerate anything less from me. I needed to have a school uniform without holes. My black shoes were totally worn out and so small by now that it was painful to wear them.

*

I made my plans this time without Yamkela and even without Atie. I did not want to get either of them involved in what I was about to do. Yamkela might have joined me just to help me out – and Atie, of course, because he loved adventures. But this thing, I had to pull through on my own.

Something I had learnt at school was: before you do something, think about it. Before you start to act, practise first. So I did.

I was spending hours and hours in our big shopping centre called Longbeach Mall, which is only a 30-minute walk from Masiphumelele. I did nothing there other than watching. Watching and more watching.

Where do the security guys patrol? What do they look out for? How to get in the shop without being noticed and, even more important, how to get out again? Which shops are crowded enough? Which are just too small and too controlled? How are the goods protected? Do they have those plastic patches on that make the alarm go off if you walk out without having them removed? Is it better to do the job with others or alone?

Always, I did it alone. Although by that time, I knew most of the gangs of little *tsotsis*. All of them just as hungry as me. I felt it was better to work alone. You might feel more protected with others, and you could develop different strategies to divert the attention of the security guys. But it always attracts their interest if they see a group of kids, some of them barefoot, entering a shop; how would they ever pay?

I can't talk about what I did in detail, except to say that. But I honestly never did steal any luxuries. And I never did it in any of the smaller shops. I only stole in the big places, like super-markets. I walked in and took a trolley like a real customer. I never ran, and I never panicked. I always checked carefully where the security guys were and whether I was out of sight of the cameras. Then I hid what I took under my clothes, especially my big sweater with the huge pockets that Mavusi had given me – or put it in a new plastic bag that I had bought for twenty cents.

I got away with it for almost three years. In all that time, I never did it with anybody else. I always told Atie, when I gave him something: 'It's from my auntie.' Or, when she wasn't around: 'Please, don't ask, Atie!'

And I always shared with him if I got something. When he started at the high school a year after me, I stole two new light-blue shirts with long sleeves for him. The real good ones, from Ackermans. Not the cheap ones from PEP. I was so happy to see him so happy . . .

I only got caught once. That was the time, towards the end of the third year, when I tried to assist Modise, one of the smaller kids who also wanted to do it alone and not within a gang. Modise was about nine at the time and urgently needed some shoes. It was in the middle of winter and he was still running around barefoot.

'Let's try PEP,' he suggested.

'Never in my life!' I laughed. 'If you go with me, you go for quality. We will try Ackermans first!'

'But we did it before in PEP, it's easy there . . .' Modise objected.

'Do you want to learn something new or not?' I interrupted him firmly.

I measured the size of his dirty feet. He looked at me with admiration and sat down on a bench about ten metres away while I entered the store.

I passed a sleepy security guard and walked confidently to the back of the shop where the shoe section was. Another rule: if you have stolen successfully, don't return too soon to the same shop. I hadn't been in that store for months. Nobody took any notice of me. I saw nice warm boots for Modise, that even had a kind of fur inside so that he would not need any socks. It was easy to tear off the alarm patch.

They were just a little too big to put under my thick jacket. But there was no other way. I squeezed the shoes under my sweater and closed the zip of the jacket. No camera could see me. But when I glanced at myself in the mirror it was obvious that such a big tummy did not fit my otherwise slim body. What to do?

There was just one way: be patient. The other customers wouldn't care. Only the sales staff and the security guy were a danger to me. I waited until the sales lady in the shoe section went to the storeroom to check something and the cashier was busy with another customer. Then I sauntered slowly to the entrance. The guard was still sleepy but was watching the entrance closely.

I could not wait much longer.

This was where I needed Modise. Fortunately, he had already noticed me from his bench. I nodded slightly and, as a natural talent, he knew what I meant. He stood up and walked towards the security guy. When he tried to walk into the shop, the guard, as expected, stopped him.

'*Suka* – go away, boy!' he shouted. Modise protested a bit, then ran off, pretending to be angry. His little show was diversion enough for me to get out unnoticed. We met in front of KFC as agreed and walked out of the mall together. Then we ran to the other side of the street. Only when we were safely behind the BP garage did I show him the shoes.

'*Enkos' buthi* – thank you, brother!' Modise said, and I could see how happy he was. He pulled on the new shoes and ran joyfully up to the toilets and back.

'*Zintle* – so beautiful!' It was not easy to calm him down.

For me that would have been enough. But then Modise made a big mistake. He wanted to do something for me now. He took off the new boots and put them into a secret place behind the toilets. 'Let me also show you something at PEP, Mbu!'

I knew it was wrong. Never return to a place of action too soon. The store he'd chosen was much too close to the one I'd just been in. Rule number two: never do something when you are excited. Modise was much too excited.

But somehow this little guy was such a warm, smart boy that I agreed to follow him back to the mall. I thought he would try to get a small chocolate or something for us from the display counters near the cashiers. This was quite an easy job – and I trusted that Modise would not make a mistake.

But he made a crazy mistake. Just for me.

While he went into the store, I waited outside for him, sitting on one of the benches, as he had done previously. I already did not like it when I saw him disappearing into the clothing section at the back of the shop. It was about two minutes later that I heard people shouting and Modise ran like a rabbit, zigzagging out of the shop. He had jammed something under his sweater but I could not see what it was. He managed to pass the guard, but then an elderly man grabbed him by the arm, not far from where I was still sitting on the bench.

Professional that he was, little Modise did not look at me. Only now did I see what he had hidden under his sweater. When the man gave him a smack against his head, he stumbled and a pair of new black shoes fell on the floor. Much too big for Modise. About my size.

I stood up and went up to the elderly man and the guard, who was now holding Modise firmly by the arm.

'He stole it for me,' I said to them calmly. They looked at me in surprise. The same instant, I pulled Modise free of the guard and shouted: '*Baleka, baleka* – run, run!'

Modise ran for his life. But it was not our lucky day. He was caught again at the entrance to the mall by one of the Nedbank guards. Together we were brought downstairs into a kind of interrogation room, where one of the security guys phoned the police.

To protect Modise, I said: 'Please, Sir, let the little one go. I forced him to steal. Otherwise I would have beaten him up . . .'

The man looked at us in disgust. 'So young – and already such criminals!'

But he allowed Modise, who looked more like seven than his real age of nine, to leave. Modise played his role perfectly and did not even look at me when he left.

I then asked one of the men if I could use the toilet. He escorted me to one of the toilets, keeping a firm hold on my arm. As we passed the doors to the underground parking lot, I suddenly punched as hard as I could with my free fist into his balls. Then I jumped through the door into the parking area and ran and ran as fast as I could.

The guard blew his whistle and used his walkie-talkie to alert the other security guys at the parking exit. But I wasn't that stupid. Instead, I opened one of the lattice ventilation grids and climbed out through it. It opened onto the area at the back of the mall, where there was always lots of chaos with delivery trucks coming and going. It was easy to run from there unnoticed to our secret place close to the BP garage toilets.

And yes – there was Modise, holding his new boots in his hands, crying.

'Put them on, man!' I said.
'You are a real friend, Mbu!' he answered, still sobbing.
'You, too, Modise!'

*

From that day on, I gave up stealing. It had been too much of a close call and I knew I would be pushing my luck if I continued. Mr Mafrika, our principal, would never allow me to continue at school if I was found to be a thief and charged with shoplifting.

But going to school hungry and in a torn uniform wasn't easy. There were times when I could not even stay at Atie's place because his father was around and wouldn't have approved. At my mom's shack it was worse than ever, as the small space was even more crowded since little Aphelele had joined the family. There were nights when I just walked around in *Masi*, trying to avoid meeting anybody as I was so ashamed of my life. Sometimes, I slept in a corner between shacks, wrapped in a blanket, trying to get away from the cold wind.

The worst night was when I couldn't find anywhere to sleep and a heavy downpour began. The only shelter I could think of was the row of small, stinky public toilets, where I locked myself in. It was so small that my back was against the door and my legs were up on the toilet. I don't know how I could fall asleep there. But I did. When I woke up, the bad smell made me vomit. I felt just so bad, so horrible. So much like shit myself.

That was the first time I wasn't sure whether I really wanted to continue with my life. I thought: enough is enough. Maybe death is better than this life. Who knows? Maybe.

8

Hope with *Gogo*
iThemba noGogo

Still, whatever happened, I did not miss a day of school. Every day after school, I changed my clothes and gave Atie my school uniform. Atie then washed and ironed it for me, since I had no place to do it myself. Every morning I picked it up and left my other clothes in a plastic bag with him, so that nobody could see how my real life was.

It was Atie who kept me going: '*Linda* – just wait, Mbu! One day, we'll live in a real, big house, with a big garden and even a big pool . . .!'

When he saw my skeptical face, he punched me in the stomach and said: 'And with many, many girls, of course!'

But for now, things got a lot worse.

*

From time to time, I was still visiting my mother, Anam, Aphelele and Anam's father. It was always good when Auntie Nompumelelo was also around, as she was never moody and always greeted me kindly. She also was one of the few in the yard who didn't drink and who looked after her own children properly – and, sometimes, also after Anam and Aphelele.

She once said to me: 'Mbu – never judge a person from the surface. Nobody is born an alcoholic or a *tikkop*. Even your mother and Siya have their own story that explains why they are the way they are today . . .'

'But why do they have children then, *Makazi*?'

'Maybe because they also didn't ask to be born . . .' she answered. I liked her for such wisdom.

As with Yamkela's mother, she always shared her food with me when I was hungry, even when she herself did not have much.

One afternoon, I went by to see her because school had finished early due to a teacher's union meeting. My aunt did not welcome me in the usual way. She looked down when I greeted her and I could see that she had been crying.

'*Makazi* – what has happened?'

But she just shook her head and gestured towards my mom's shack at the back.

Deeply worried, I hurried over there. Inside, I found the whole family: my mother, Anam, Aphelele and even Anam's father. He had not gone to work as he usually did at this time of day.

When my mom saw me, she stood up and embraced me, as she hadn't done since I was very small. Then she started crying in a loud, high voice that sent shivers down my spine.

'*Mama, nceda* – please, what has happened?' I still had no clue.

Then she cried loudly: '*Ufile* – he is dead . . . Mavusi, your brother Mavusi, is dead!'

Mavusi, Mavusi, Mavusi . . . my hero brother from the days of my childhood. Since he was four years older than me, he must have been nineteen by now. My only blood brother. For God's sake – what had happened?

Intoni – what? An accident, a murder, a killing disease? What?

Finally, my mother wiped her nose and explained it to me:

'Mavusi had TB for a long time, as we all know. He had it even as a child. But something went wrong with his brain recently. He got more and more confused. He could not speak complete sentences anymore. He could not even find his way home, and ran all the time after papers the wind blew in front of him . . .'

'But why did nobody tell me earlier?' I asked, starting to sob. At last the terrible truth of my older brother's death had reached my heart. He was the one who had looked after me when nobody else in my family did. When I was still so small, when he was still so small, he took care of me.

My mother continued: 'Last night he got a high fever. *Gogo* gave called the ambulance at about midnight, but nobody came. By this morning, Mavusi was dead. Maybe his lungs gave up, maybe his heart. Maybe both . . . The funeral will be next Saturday in Graaff Reinet.'

I don't know why I was always so convinced that one day my brother and I would be reunited again. I had never given up on him, although we'd hardly had any contact since I had left him behind in *Gogo*'s house a few years back. He was refusing to speak to me then, already. Maybe it was the medication, even then, that made him so changed?

'I will not go to the funeral . . .' Siya said, without anybody asking him.

My mother said: 'We have a relative in Worcester who phoned to say that she will pay for our transport . . . for me and you, Mbu. Will you come?'

I nodded my head. There was no doubt that I would go. I wanted to say goodbye to Mavusi. I wanted to be at my brother's funeral at all costs.

*

Yamkela lent me a white shirt, a tie and even a dark-brown jacket. Atie walked with us to the bus station on Friday afternoon, carrying my mom's bag. The little ones stayed behind with Auntie Nompumelelo and Anam's father.

I sat sleepless while the bus drove through the night, thinking about the last time I'd travelled this route, coming from the other direction. Would I have the chance to see Mrs Naki again? How would *Gogo* receive me? Would our father come to the funeral?

When I asked mom about our father coming, she said: 'He has been told about the funeral by that relative of ours from Worcester . . . I don't know whether he will be there.'

The way she said it left no doubt that she did not want to meet him there at all.

There were many people at the funeral, maybe seventy or more. My father was not among them. As a blood brother I was allowed to look into the coffin before it was finally closed. Mavusi's face was so familiar, but at the same time so strange, and very old. He looked like someone of sixty. He was so skinny that you could see every bone in his face and his closed eyes seemed sunken into his skull.

I tried to feel something towards him, but I couldn't. It was as if he was gone long ago, already. This was not Mavusi anymore. This was just a coffin with a dead body. The soul of Mavusi was long gone to our ancestors . . . I felt so sad to realise that we wouldn't ever be united in this life anymore.

*

Gogo greeted me much more kindly than I had expected. '*Uxolo* – sorry, Mbu. I know how much your brother always meant to you.'

'*Enkosi, Gogo* – thank you,' I responded, and took her hand. I hadn't realised she had even noticed during those years that I was in her house.

As the proceedings of the day went on, I searched ever more urgently for Mrs Naki and her siblings, Ayanda and Andiswa, but none of them was among the guests.

'Oh, the Naki family,' *Gogo* said, when I finally asked. 'All three of them left for Mthatha a long time ago . . .'

The news made me very despondent. I felt so lonely when all the others began to eat the rice, cabbage salad and grilled chicken served to the funeral guests that I couldn't join in. Back in *Masi* I was always so hungry; here, I couldn't eat a piece of anything.

Why had my father not come, although there were several relatives from his side at the funeral? Probably, he would also not have come if it was me who had died.

I tried to speak to some of my father's relatives about him but they didn't want to talk. Only one uncle befriended me: 'I am your mother's brother, and so your blood uncle,' he said. 'I am as poor as your parents, but I am not drinking. My name is Vukile . . .'

'*Uhlala phi, Malume* – where do you stay, Uncle?'

'In an informal settlement near Ottery, in *iKapa*,' was his answer.

I had never heard of this settlement before. When I asked him for his cell number, he wrote it for me on a small piece of paper. I kept it safe for many years. It was good to know about him, even though I didn't phone him. Maybe I would contact him one day . . .

The next morning we took a bus back to *iKapa*. Sitting in the rumbling bus for all those hours, watching the scenery pass, I realised how much I had missed Yamkela and Atie.

*

It was after dark when we arrived back in *Masi*. I said goodbye to my mom and headed straight for Atie's place. It was already late by that time, and since there was no light in his father's shack, I went straight to our little palace. I wanted to tell him everything about my brother's funeral.

It was also dark in the caravan but the nearby street light made it easy to find your way. The moment I opened the unlocked door and stumbled inside, I felt that something was different. There was somebody else sleeping in our bed next to Atie, but I could not make out who.

'Atie?' I said uncertainly.

At first, there was no movement at all. I called his name a second time and touched the blanket where his feet were. The other person was fully covered by the blanket, even the head, and did not move at all.

Finally, Atie's head and shoulders appeared: '*Uxolo* – sorry, Mbu, it just happened . . .'

I still wasn't sure what was going on. But I felt really stupid.

'She just joined me, you know . . .' There was a pause, and then he continued: 'It's Unathi.'

Of course I knew Unathi. She was much older than Atie, even a bit older than me. A cute girl, and a sexy one. But I have to tell you, Unathi was also trouble.

We all knew that she'd done 'it' many times already. And when she was drunk or on *tik*, she did it with everybody, for another drink or some food.

'Does your dad know?' I said to Atie.

'Are you crazy?'

'Will she stay the whole night?'

'Come on, Mbu, it's just this one night. She's really good. I even gave her cash.'

Then he said what only Atie could have said: 'Do you also want? I can ask her and wait outside . . .'

63

That was Atie. How could I be angry? For a moment I really didn't know what to do. Is sharing a girl like sharing clothes or food? This Unathi was really cute, no question. I don't think she was stupid, either. I'd heard stories that she always had condoms with her and demanded that the guys used them. But what about when she was really drunk or on *tik*?

I stood there gazing at my friend Atie. He looked stronger than me, even though he was so much younger and smaller; I could see the muscles on his arms and shoulders. He was patiently waiting for my response to his offer.

At last I shook my head. '*Ndidiniwe* – I'm just too tired, Atie. I've spent too many hours in the bus. Maybe next time . . .'

I took my small bag and went out, closing the door from the outside. Through all of this I had not even seen Unathi. But I knew that Atie would never lie to me about something so important.

Somehow, I felt that this had been something important. A new and important stage in our lives. But only if you understood what it meant. I didn't really get it at the time.

*

That night was another one without a roof over my head. And the next day was the first that I was late for school, because I had slept too long under some cardboard sheets on the outskirts of the wetlands. Even worse was that Atie had not washed my uniform from the previous week, so I returned this Monday with dirty clothes and a bad smell on my body.

Our teacher in Grade 8 was Mrs Mhlana, an elderly woman who was always dressed like a lady. Despite her age she wore high heels and a heavy necklace with a gold cross.

She treated all of us with a special respect. 'You can reach for the stars . . .' she'd encourage us, when we were tired or somebody had not done their homework. 'Don't accept darkness. God is light and you, as children of God, can touch the light!'

That morning, she'd seen immediately that I was in bad shape. When I entered the classroom, she greeted me as 'Mister Maloni!' – and nobody laughed. I bowed my head and mumbled: 'Sorry, so sorry . . .'

She continued with the lesson: isiXhosa literature. Modern literature by women like Sindiwe Magona. What a beautiful sound! Usually I loved listening to her reading to us. But this morning, somehow, I could not concentrate.

During the break she asked me to carry her heavy bag, full of books, to the staffroom. When we were far away from the others, she looked at me and said: 'You are in trouble, Mbu, aren't you?'

I did not look back at her. With my eyes downcast I answered: 'No, Mrs Mhlana, all is fine.'

*

After school I was so hungry that I wasn't sure how much longer I could resist going back to Longbeach Mall, to one of the big shops; just once more. I managed to keep resisting. But it was hard. I was starving. I lost weight as if I had the dreaded disease. But it was nothing more than hunger that ate at me. Finally, I just couldn't hold out anymore. I knew that I was on the point of going back to the old ways of getting food without paying.

It was Yamkela who saved me from further trouble. I was on my way back from school when I heard him calling my name from the other side of the busy Pokela Road. We greeted each other and he invited me home with him to have some sandwiches. I was so hungry that I could hardly control myself and once we were sitting down in their living room, I just ate and ate and ate. I ate so much and so fast that a few minutes later I felt a rush of nausea and just made it to the toilet in time to vomit.

'You are too skinny, Mbu!' Yamkela said, as I walked slowly back in from the toilet.

I wanted to apologise to him for my behaviour, but I couldn't say a word. I could only look at him in deep despair, and would have probably started crying like in old times; but there were no more tears left in me, so I just kept looking at him, like a beaten dog.

We sat there and did not speak a word. Later, Yamkela started to play music on his small keyboards. He was playing music I'd never heard before. Maybe he had just composed it. Maybe for me.

Yamkela will be a famous musician one day, I guarantee it. Nobody taught him anything, but he's very good. His mom brought the keyboards back one day from the old age home and Yamkela started playing it. He's been playing ever since.

The sun was going down. I watched it through the window of Yamkela's brick house. The many poor shacks in the neighbourhood seemed like little matchbox houses, like toys, all painted red and orange by the late sunlight.

It was dark when Yamkela stopped playing and said to me: 'Do you want to go with me to Ta Simpra's youth group tonight?'

'What?'

'Ta Simpra runs a youth group at the HOKISA Peace House in Kanana Road. They have it once a week. They talk about Aids and drugs and at the end there is bread and juice for everybody . . .'

There was nothing better I had to do, so I went with Yamkela to the meeting.

*

I had expected that Ta Simpra would be an older man, someone well respected, since this is what the title 'Ta' indicated. But he turned out to be a young man in his late twenties, a born youth leader who could really listen and wanted us to talk about the things that troubled us in our lives. While I'd felt embarrassed when my teacher, Mrs Mhlana, had asked me about my trouble, I now listened with open ears to what others had to say. The serious topic this evening was teenage pregnancy. I could hardly believe my eyes when I saw Unathi there – not drunk at all. She was quiet like I was, but seemed to be listening with equal attention.

Ta Simpra spoke about his own youth when he had to look after younger siblings, and I was reminded of Mavusi when I heard him speaking. He told us that he worked in HOKISA, which stands for Homes for Kids in South Africa. It is a small Children's Home in *Masi* that caters for kids in our community who have lost their parents to HIV/Aids – or whose parents are not able to look after them. I had heard about this place but had always avoided it, as I did not want to get too close to any kind of social workers. The only ones I knew so far worked for the court in Simon's Town and went looking for the parents of the young *tsotsis* who were caught at Longbeach Mall.

It was only after Atie said he would join me that I agreed to visit this place called HOKISA Children's Home. Atie, as always, was game for the new and unknown: 'What do we have to lose?' he argued. 'You can't go on sleeping on the streets whenever my dad's around. Maybe you can get a bed at this place.'

So we went there one afternoon. Ta Simpra had arranged for us to meet some of the senior people working there, including one of the directors, an older white guy. As always in new situations, I was quiet at first and it was Atie who spoke.

'I am worried about Mbu,' he said. 'He gets so down sometimes. He can't go on living like a dog. Worse than a dog. And he is a better person than me – Mbu really wants to go to school!'

'Is that true?' the white director asked me. I nodded my head.

'Come and see us again, okay? I'll talk to Ta Simpra. He'll speak to your mother and then we'll let you know . . .' the director said.

Three days later we were called back. Unfortunately, there was no bed available at the Children's Home, but Ta Simpra had spoken to my mother and my Aunt Nompumelelo, and had even phoned *Gogo* back in Masizakhe to check if I could go and stay with her again.

'You know the problem here in *Masi*; your people just don't have space for you . . . and it also doesn't go so well with your stepfather, right?' Ta Simpra began. How had he got to know all that in such a short time?

He then asked me: 'What is most important to you in your life, Mbu?'

I did not hesitate for a second: 'I want to finish school . . . I want to get my Matric!' Atie nodded his head in support.

Then Ta Simpra said calmly: 'I phoned your *Gogo*. She would be willing to allow you to stay in her house until you have passed Grade 12 . . . what do you think?'

Back to *Gogo* in Masizakhe? I wasn't sure. On the other hand, my life here in *iKapa* was becoming more and more unbearable. And at least *Gogo* had been okay at Mavusi's funeral.

'Can I think about it?' I asked.

'Of course . . .' Ta Simpra responded.

When we were back in the street, Atie knocked at his forehead: 'You are funny, man. You are the smartest of all of us. If any of us can get a Matric, it's you. How can you spoil this offer?'

*

By the next day I'd made up my mind. I would go back to *Gogo*. I would be strong. I needed to eat to be able to learn properly.

My teacher Mrs Mhlana wrote an encouraging letter to the school in Graaff Reinet, urging them to accept me into the next grade – Grade 10.

It felt as if there were, for the first time, good people out there who were really on my side.

The director of the Children's Home paid for my bus ticket and even took me to the station in his old car. I promised to write him a letter at the end of my first month in the new school.

I was hopeful that I would work something out with *Gogo*. I was even prepared to join her at church on Sundays. I was prepared to give back.

9

Months in prison
Inyanga etilongweni

All those hours on the bus to Masizakhe I was in a happy
mood. Maybe life would be good to me this time?

Ta Simpra and his colleagues at the Children's Home had
given me snacks and a bottle of juice for the trip. Yamkela had
recorded some of his fantastic gospel music for me and, through
Atie, someone else had given me a second-hand set of headphones
so I could listen to it all the way . . .

The HOKISA director – whom I called Doc like the others did,
although he was not a medical doctor – had handed me R200 in
cash before we arrived at the bus station. 'That's for your new
school uniform in Masizakhe!' he said.

I thanked him and put it deep in my pocket.

'I can trust you, Mbu?' he asked.

'You can, Doc,' I answered, looking him straight in the eyes.
I'd never met people before who cared for me like these guys, Ta
Simpra and the Doc, did. Never would I disappoint them.

*

The day was already warm by the time the bus drew into Graaff
Reinet early the next morning. It was the end of January and the

new term had started. I was intending to have a quick wash and then go straight to my new school to register. Afterwards I would go and buy my new uniform, so as to be ready for a good start the following day.

I walked confidently from the taxi rank to *Gogo*'s house. It all still felt familiar to me, even though so many years had passed and I was now so much bigger and, yes, also more mature than the last time I'd been here. The front door stood wide open, but I knocked politely anyway.

'*Ngena* – come in, Mbu!' I heard *Gogo* call from one of the bedrooms.

'*Molo, Gogo*,' I greeted her cautiously. There was no one else there. All the other kids had left for school already.

When she came out of the bedroom into the light of the living room, I could see that she was not in a good mood. I hoped it was not because of me.

'The Welfare people have not approved the foster grants for two of the youngest kids I've just accepted,' she said in a grumpy voice. 'What do they think? That I am a millionaire?'

I thought it might be better to leave her alone for the moment. I did not ask where I could sleep but put my bag down next to the door, took my shirt off and went to the bathroom to wash myself.

I had just started to pour cold water over my head when she came in and addressed me aggressively: '*Mamela* – listen! This guy from the Children's Home promised that they would send money with you. How much did they give you?'

I took my head out from under the water and looked at her in concern: '*Hayi, Gogo* – the only money I've received is for my new uniform . . .'

'How much?' she asked again, impatiently.

'Just R200 . . . I need all of it for the uniform,' I repeated.

'*Bububhanxa* – nonsense!' she shouted angrily. 'In the old days you could make do with a second-hand one. Are you Mister Special now?'

I did not know what else to say. This should have been a good start, but it didn't seem like it. I remembered my promise to the Doc that I would try. I would not bow down to her bad mood today.

I finished washing and then got ready to go to the new school and, afterwards, buy the uniform as planned. I left my bag with the rest of my belongings next to the entrance.

Gogo did not answer when I said: '*Sobonana, Gogo* – see you later.'

*

The school secretary was a young woman who seemed to recognise me from the old times: '*Goh* – you are a real man now, Mbu!'

'Not yet!' I answered with a smile. Here, at least, I felt welcome.

'See you tomorrow. We start at eight,' she told me after I had completed all the forms. 'Grade 10 is in the grey building opposite the yard . . .' She pointed it out to me.

From there I went to the PEP store nearby and bought all that I needed, even underwear and some extra t-shirts. From the rest of the money I purchased a small mint chocolate, as I knew that this had always been *Gogo*'s favourite.

It was early evening when I returned home and all the other kids were around. Some greeted me in a friendly way, others just ignored me. *Gogo* acted as if she did not see me.

When bedtime came, I still didn't know where I was going to sleep. There were no spare beds in *Gogo*'s house. Not a serious problem; I was prepared to share like in the old days.

Before long everybody was in bed and *Gogo*, too, had withdrawn to her room. She still had not spoken to me, not a single word. I had just begun to put a blanket down on the floor of the living room when one of the boys came out again and talked to me in a low voice: '*Usandikhumbula* – do you remember me? I am Ababalwe, one of *Gogo*'s grandchildren . . .'

Yes, I knew his name and, indeed, I remembered little Ababalwe. When I'd last seen him he was not even at school yet.

'How old are you now, Ababalwe?' I asked him.

'Twelve!' he answered proudly. I did not tell him that I'd thought he was ten at the most.

He offered to share his bed with me and I accepted gratefully. I fell asleep almost immediately.

*

The next morning, *Gogo* was still not speaking to me. I knew from experience that her bad moods could sometimes last for several days. But then suddenly they would be over. Like blue sky reappearing after a bad storm.

Before I left for school, while she was dressing in the bathroom, I put the small mint chocolate on the little cupboard next to her bed. I left without even a goodbye from her.

This silent treatment went on for another two days. I was allowed to eat with the others, but she refused to talk to me. What was she thinking all that time? Was she making plans to get rid of me?

By the third day, I'd started thinking that I might have to look for another place to stay. Maybe at the end of the week I would speak to my new teacher, a young man from Zimbabwe, and see if he could help. If I could have known what was coming, I would not have waited even one day longer. By the time I came home from school on the third day, it was all too late already . . .

*

As I turned the corner into our street, I wondered why a police van was parked there, close to *Gogo*'s house. But as there were no blue lights flashing and no crowd standing around it, I did not suspect anything.

I walked home slowly, feeling hungry and a bit tired after the long day at school. So much was still new to me there. I not only had to get to know the teachers and all the other learners, but several of the subjects were taught differently to the way I was used to.

I had reached the house and was walking through the garden when a grey-haired police officer appeared at the door, with *Gogo* beside him.

'That's him!' she said, pointing her thin finger towards me.

The policeman walked up to me while *Gogo* waited at the door. I didn't make a move. I still had no clue what was going on.

A second policeman, younger than the first, appeared behind *Gogo* and stood looking at me curiously. Only now did I realise that no other kids were around. They must have all been ordered into the house.

The first policeman had reached me now. Without a word, he grabbed my arm and put handcuffs around my wrists. Then he said, in an official manner: 'Mbu Maloni, you are arrested.'

I could not believe what I was hearing. I was sure I had done nothing wrong since my return to Masizakhe.

I started shouting: 'But why? I have done nothing!'

The younger policeman joined us and they shoved me towards their van. The older one unlocked the back door and they both pushed me in roughly.

'You know very well what you've done!' the younger officer said to me, with an ugly grin on his face.

The older one turned the ignition key and the motor rumbled to life. Over the noise, he shouted into the back of the car:

'You have abused that little boy who was kind enough to share his bed with you – you are a rapist!'

It was as if someone had knocked me on the head with a heavy hammer. This was beyond my worst imagination. There was only one person who could have invented this story, and she had done it out of revenge . . .

*

The rest of that day, not much more happened. I was photo-graphed and my fingerprints were taken. I had to sign some forms. Not all of them made sense to me. At the police station was a cell, where I was locked up. I had to spend the night with an old, fat, very drunk guy who snored the whole time and did not speak to me at all.

The whole of the next day, I just stayed in the cell. On the third day, I was taken to a court not far away. The presiding magistrate was what we called a *boer*, a white Afrikaner, who looked at me with disgust. He explained the charges against me in Afrikaans, and they were then translated into isiXhosa by an interpreter. But I'd understood what was said anyway as I was not bad in Afrikaans at school.

I was accused of having raped Ababalwe during the night. And threatening to beat him if he told anybody. I was sure that he would never have invented this story by himself.

The magistrate paged through some documents for a while. Then, finally, he said to me: 'Guilty or not?'

I knew I had to be strong and stand up for myself. I looked at him and answered in Afrikaans: '*Nie skuldig nie* – not guilty!'

He made no response to my answer, just scribbled some notes on a piece of paper and gestured to one of the policemen to take me out. I was escorted out to a police van, but it did not drive back to the police station. Instead, it took one of the roads leading out of Graaff Reinet. I saw signs to PE.

PE is what we call *iBhayi* – Port Elizabeth, a big harbour town in the Eastern Cape.

By the time we arrived at the outskirts of PE a few hours later, my back felt painful from the long drive in the uncomfortable van. We pulled up at a modern-looking place with high walls around it that had barbed wire on top. I didn't know it then but this was Enkuselweni, the juvenile prison for awaiting-trial prisoners, young guys of between fifteen and twenty years old. I had turned seventeen just a month before . . .

*

The policemen escorted me in. We had to pass through a few security doors, with lots of cameras and armed guards. I had to empty all my pockets and sign yet another form. Other than that, I could keep my normal clothes. I was then brought to a big cell with many other prisoners in it, some younger, some older than me. The door was locked again behind me. There were about fifty of us, just in our cell. I saw that some had their gang names tattooed on their arms and hands, and one even had it on his neck.

One of the older guys tapped me on my shoulder as I was trying to find a place next to the wall: '*Uzotini apha* – what are you here for?'

Everybody was watching us. He had a tattoo of the *ama26* on the top of his hand. *Ama26* are the robbery gangs, as *ama28* is for those who do rape. I knew that one wrong word or one wrong move could be fatal – or at least cause serious trouble for me. Right now, at this moment . . . or later, tonight.

'Shoplifting!' I answered, looking straight back at the other boy.

'*Phaya* – there!' he pointed to a dirty but empty mattress across the way.

Fortunately, I knew some of the prison language from the gangs in Masiphumelele. Although we had never been a member of any of them, Atie and I had listened often to their stories in some of the *shebeens*. They spoke in a mixture of isiZulu, isiXhosa, Afrikaans and other languages, as the migrant workers do in the mines.

The law of the cells was: if you belonged to the right gang, you would be safe. If you belonged to the wrong one, you should start praying . . .

As the older guy had the gang name *ama26* on his hand, there was hope for me. I knew some of their code words. It seemed as if the *ama26* were ruling this cell, not any of the others, like the *ama27* or *ama28*.

I had just sat down on the mattress when a group of guys approached me. Their leader, a well-built guy with a shaven head and tattoos of naked girls on his chest, said in a low voice: '*Phakama* – get up!'

I stood up, and knew the moment had come.

His face was close to mine when he whispered: '*Ngawuth' bathi ugubani* – who are you?'

As it was clear by now that the *ama26* were in charge here, I knew what was expected in reply. I responded in an equally low voice with their code: '*Ndiyimpumalanga.*' What that literally means is, 'I come from the east, the sunrise'. But in gang code the meaning is much more complicated.

My interrogator pushed me back onto the mattress and spoke in a voice that everybody could hear: '*Kulungile* – all right, boy, follow our rules. You will be okay then.'

77

We had to go for supper at about six o'clock. At exactly seven o'clock all of us were locked into the cells again.

That was the first day out of exactly one hundred and fifty-eight days that I spent in that cell. That's almost six months. In prison, most people count every day. I did the same.

*

The days were tough. But the nights were horror. I had already realised how important it was to know the right codes. I thank God that I was able to give the correct response when tested. Others were less lucky.

There were different punishments. Heavy ones and light ones. Those from the guards and those from the other inmates. The ones from the other boys were by far the most cruel.

The cell space was clearly demarcated: the best area was occupied by the *ama26*. Second best and considerably smaller, was the area of *ama28*. The rest was open territory. Everybody knew exactly where the borders were. The lights were left on all night, so there was no way to ignore what was going on.

Normally after supper, most of the guys just withdrew to their beds. Some would sleep or pretend to sleep; some would be reading soccer magazines; some working on each other's tattoos. Others did business: they dealt *dagga* or agreed on certain actions for later in the night. Once we were locked up for the night, the guards normally did not interfere with whatever was going on.

That first night I was nervous. Although I still felt relatively safe, I tried to make myself as invisible as possible. When the guy in the bunk bed above me started to chat about his many girlfriends, I responded with only a yes or no . . . and pretended to be tired. He finally found somebody else to talk to. Much later, I somehow managed to fall asleep.

I woke up because of the screaming of somebody. It had been only one horrible long scream; then somebody else pressed a towel in the face of the poor guy who, other than that first scream, did not oppose those handling him anymore. Never had I seen anything so brutal: about five or six guys were holding down another boy who lay bent forward over a table with his bare back exposed, not far from me. They had stripped his pants down and pulled his shirt up. Why him, I don't know. He was not even one of the smallest. Probably my age.

As I woke up, one of the older ones, also naked around the waist, had just stepped back from him and pulled up his pants. He was laughing and shouted: '*Olandelayo* – next!' Another guy opened his pants and started to rape the poor guy on the table. Most of the other inmates were watching, although some, like me, pretended to be still asleep.

I had pulled the blanket over my head, but still kept watching through almost closed eyes. What a nightmare! But this was no bad dream. This was happening in front of me . . . and I had no idea what to do, except pray that they would never get me. Some nights there were more rapes than beatings. Some nights there were more beatings.

*

I admit that even today, I still cannot talk – or write – about everything that happened during those many nights in the PE prison. Maybe one day I'll be able to speak about it. But right now, it's too painful. Even when I just think about it, my heart starts beating too fast. I get anxious and can't concentrate.

The days were more controlled than the nights. Partly it was because the prison warders were around then. But also, daylight hours were when the *ama26* ruled. So the *ama28* activities did not go on then.

We had to get up and wash ourselves at 6.00 a.m. Breakfast was at 7.00 a.m. Then there was school, in small classes, from 8.00 until 14.00. No easy job for those poor teachers. Most of the other boys refused to learn anything. I kept quiet as much as possible, only speaking when called on by the teacher. I never raised my hand.

In the afternoons we were allowed out into the courtyard, supervised by some of the educators, and the guards, of course. It was there that I met Sivu, who was one of the *ama28*. Thanks to him I joined a soccer team, and since I was not bad at soccer, became more accepted by the others, including those who were not *ama26*.

I was still waiting for my day in court, but it was postponed and postponed again. Finally, a young black lawyer visited me. That was the first good experience I had in almost two months. He asked me questions and listened, and made notes about what I said. After he left, I thought: *mhlawumbi* . . . maybe . . . he really believes me.

Then I had my first day in court, which lasted not longer than ten minutes. The judge postponed everything again, as there was conflicting evidence. Aside from the young lawyer, a social worker also began visiting me from time to time. She was a really nice coloured lady called Karen. She asked me whether she could do anything for me. I asked if she could arrange for me to phone Ta Simpra or the Doc. I was wondering the whole time whether they had heard back in Masiphumelele what had happened to me here.

The next day, I was called to Karen's office again. She said the Doc would phone me there and we just had to wait. Not long after, the phone rang and, indeed, it was Doc. I was so excited to hear his voice that I could only say: 'Help me, please help me to get out of here!'

He promised to make sure that a social worker from Masiphumelele would phone Karen soon to organise more support for me.

From that day on I had some hope again. About a week later I was able to speak to the social worker, Nomfuneko, from *Masi*. She told me that she was trying to find a place for me to come back to since *Gogo* was still claiming that I was a rapist and had even told that to my mom and my auntie. Would they really believe her – or me?

When the Soccer World Cup kicked off in South Africa on 11 June 2010, I was still in prison. We were allowed to watch most of the games on TV. Probably because the guards also did not want to miss anything. I cheered along with the others for our team, Bafana Bafana. When they were knocked out in the first round, I chose Spain as my favourite. There was a lot of betting going on and I could have earned some good cash. But deep in my heart, I was just so sad. When I saw all the people on TV cheering in the beautiful stadiums all over South Africa, I thought: look at me . . . sitting here in this ugly place with all these cruel guys. The beatings and the rapes continued even during the World Cup.

More time went by. But at least I knew now that I was not forgotten. That thought kept me going. That and the knowledge that there were still a few people who did not believe *Gogo*'s story.

*

Finally, early one morning in July, my lawyer arrived and told me to put my stuff together.

'We have a good chance. It's probable that judgment will be given today. I've got a report by a reputable doctor who will testify . . .'

When I was brought into the courtroom, I saw *Gogo* and other people from Masizakhe sitting at the back. Ababalwe was also there. I avoided looking at any of them.

Several witnesses and experts were called. The presiding judge was, once again, a *boer*; but this one was polite and treated everybody, including me, with respect.

When the medical doctor was called, he said something that contradicted clearly what *Gogo* and her grandson had accused me of. Speaking in English, he said: 'I examined the boy who had told us that he had been the victim of the accused. I examined him carefully and repeatedly. I could not find any trace of violent sexual abuse. I cannot exclude that there may have been voluntary sexual activity between the boys, but certainly not rape.'

When the court interpreter translated his statement into Afrikaans and isiXhosa, *Gogo* stood up from her seat and shouted: 'Do you say that I am a liar?'

The judge commanded her to sit down and to be quiet as she would otherwise be ordered to leave the room.

Then the judge withdrew and we all had to wait. I just prayed and did not speak to anybody. Finally, he returned and we all had to stand up.

He looked at me as he repeated all the accusations against me, and then said the words I had prayed for: 'The accused, Mbu Maloni, is acquitted of all charges.'

Half an hour later, I left the court as a free man.

'Where will you go from here?' the young lawyer asked me.

'I have no idea,' I answered. But I smiled at him as I said it. I had survived so much already. Nothing could be worse than what I'd been through.

Somehow, I would find a way to return to my friends Atie and Yamkela . . .

10

A real home
iKhaya eli lilo

Most people had already left the court but I saw that one person had stayed behind to wait for me. It was one of *Gogo*'s adult daughters, the same one who used to come to church with us all those many years ago. I wasn't sure about her intentions and approached her cautiously. But I could see that she did not look at me with hostility.

'*Uxolo* – sorry, Mbu. I am really sorry for what my mother did to you. How can I help you?'

'I need to get away from here. I want to go back to *iKapa*. But first I want to fetch my stuff from *Gogo*'s house. Can you help me with this?'

She nodded and we left the court together. She even paid my bus ticket back to Graaff Reinet. When we arrived at Masizakhe, she said: 'I will get your things from my mother's house . . . and I've organised with one of your aunts on your mother's side that you can sleep at her place until your departure . . .'

Gogo's daughter kept her word. She not only brought my stuff to me but also all the belongings of my late brother Mavusi. I was very grateful to see his clothing, even though all of it was in bad condition, dirty and torn.

I put everything in a big bag. Then I went to the house of this aunt, where I spent two nights. I wasn't sure whether she believed me or *Gogo*, but she treated me kindly. The biggest challenge was that she also had no money to help with my transport from Graaff Reinet back to Cape Town. There was only one way forward: I needed to get in touch with Ta Simpra or the Doc – and, finally, I knew what to do.

The next morning, so early that it was still dark outside, I thanked my aunt for hiding me for those two nights without telling *Gogo* or anybody else, and walked all the way to the main road to get a lift to PE. I was lucky, as one of the big trucks stopped for me about an hour later; and I was on my way back – to the prison.

The guard at the gate could hardly believe his eyes when he saw me with my big bag, ringing the bell at the main gate: 'Hey, Mbu – are you mad? I think you are the only prisoner who has ever returned here voluntarily! Did you like our food so much?'

But he opened the small door next to the gate and once I was through the metal detector check, he even allowed me a call to Karen's office. I was so lucky that she was still in, for it was late afternoon by that time.

'Please, Karen, can you phone the Doc or the social worker, Nomfuneko?' I asked her. 'I can't stay in Masizakhe anymore and I'm hoping they will help me to get back to *iKapa* . . .'

I saw that Karen really liked me. She gave me a warm smile and made a few calls to check whether I could spend a night or two in one of the visitors' rooms at the prison, until my return to *Masi* was agreed on.

Finally, the best news of all came from Karen: 'The Doc said that there is now a room available for you at the HOKISA Children's Home . . . they have accepted you, as long as we can organise your transport there. Congratulations, Mbu!'

But I was still worried: 'Who will pay for the bus ticket from PE to Cape Town?'

'I will,' Karen said, smiling at me. I also had a smile on my face. I would never judge all social workers the same way again.

A real home

Two days later, very early in the morning, one of the youth workers woke me up and brought me to the main gate. A guard from the prison drove me to the bus station and gave me the ticket. Attached was a handwritten note from Karen: 'Good luck, Mbu! Never come back!'

At six o'clock sharp the bus left, driving off into the early morning light, direction *iKapa*.

*

It was dark in Cape Town by the time the bus arrived thirteen hours later, almost on time. It had been agreed that I would wait at the terminal and that the Doc would fetch me from there in his old Toyota.

There are times in life when everything seems to go wrong. And other times when you are in the lucky draw, when things finally seem to go right . . . hopefully forever.

I still was in the lucky draw. I saw Doc before he saw me. There he was, like a father picking up his son. He carried my heavy bag over his shoulder and put it into the boot of his car. He offered me a juice while we drove.

'Hungry?' he asked.

'Yes . . . thank you.'

He gave me a sandwich and an apple. We did not speak much.

When we arrived at the Children's Home in Masiphumelele, Ta Simpra unlocked the gate for us. An icy wind was blowing. It was end of July, deep winter in the Western Cape. I had been away for more than six months.

The Doc gave me the key to the garden hut, a little brick house next to the entrance to the premises and adjacent to the doctor's surgery. The hut was one of the rooms for teenagers at the Children's Home. All the walls were painted white, and there was a cupboard, a bed with clean blankets and a small table with a lamp on it. You could still smell the fresh paint.

'I only finished preparing your room this afternoon,' Ta Simpra said.

It was close to midnight when he and the Doc left. I locked the door from the inside. Actually, I had been planning to go straight out to Yamkela or Atie, no matter how late it was. But I didn't.

I needed to stay where I was. I needed to just be for a while. I felt safe in a way I had never felt safe before. Somebody had picked me up from the station, just like that. Somebody had organised a new bed for the room and Ta Simpra had painted it only this afternoon. All for me. Not for money. Why?

I wasn't sure. I just knew something was different in my life. Something good. I liked the smell of the fresh paint and decided not to go anywhere, not tonight . . . and not anymore.

*

The next morning, I slept longer than usual. It was already daylight when somebody knocked at my door. It was one of the older boys: 'Mbu, is it you in there? Get up, man, you can join us for school . . .'

At Masiphumelele High School I was allowed to continue with Grade 10, although I had missed most of the first two terms. I promised to do extra lessons in order to catch up what I'd missed. That same afternoon, I went to Longbeach Mall to buy the light-blue and grey uniform for Masiphumelele High, with money I had received from Ta Simpra.

I bought black shoes at Ackermans – and paid proudly in cash. At PEP Store next door, I purchased trousers, two shirts and even a jacket against the wind and rain. Nobody recognised me from my last visit, long ago, when I was there with my little friend Modise. It was such a pleasure to buy, such a pleasure to do the right thing. I was tempted to change everything at the customer service counter, just for the pleasure of going through the whole procedure of buying again, like everybody else. I gave a big smile to the guard at the entrance. He smiled back, innocently, not recognising me at all.

From there I walked straight to my mother's yard. I wasn't sure what they had heard about the whole case and what *Gogo* had told them on the phone. Since Auntie Nompumelelo's shack was close to the entrance of the yard, I first knocked at her door.

She opened it and looked at me angrily. Despite the cold wind blowing outside she did not invite me in: 'Mbu – you did a wrong thing. *Suka* – go away, Mbu! We don't want to see you here anymore . . .'

I tried to stop her from closing the door and said: '*Kodwa, Makazi* – but it's not true. I did not even touch the boy . . .'

The door closed in my face. I heard her locking it with a chain from the inside. She then turned the radio on.

There was nobody at my mother's shack, not even the children.

From there I walked straight to Yamkela's. His house was locked, too. Maybe my lucky draw was over?

Although I had two big plastic bags with my uniform in my hand, I returned in a sad mood to my new home at HOKISA. When I entered through the gate, I saw two guys hiding from the rough wind in a corner – my friends Atie and Yamkela!

'Are you going to let us freeze out here forever, Mbu?' Atie shouted and I saw a big smile on both their faces.

They joined me in my little room. Atie sat on the bed, Yamkela on the only chair and me on the floor. We talked and talked, until it was dark outside . . .

I felt I was finally home, not with my family but with a kind of new family. People who cared for me.

Nobody will ever kill me

*

I have to admit that it took a few weeks before I trusted the
adults and other kids at HOKISA. I could hardly believe that they
were just kind people. Maybe they were only pretending and
one day would want me to pay them back in one way or another?
What did they think about the accusations against me as a rapist?

After a while I realised that half the township had heard the
news of my arrest in the Eastern Cape as a rapist. Since rumours
spread like fire in *Masi*, the stories became wilder and wilder:
Mbu has raped five girls; Mbu had sex with a prostitute and her
mother; Mbu is a *moffie* and has been raped by two other men;
Mbu has raped all the small boys at his school . . .

I ignored all of this nonsense. As much as possible.

But it was not easy. I sometimes saw girls of my age giggling
with each other when they saw me; when I came closer, they'd
look the other way and totally ignore me. One evening a drunk
guy followed me, shouting: '*Mamela* – listen, Mbu: how did you
have sex with the little girls? And with how many . . . hey? Was
it fun?' Others joined in his stupid laughter.

No word was spoken against me at the Children's Home. But
I was sure the older ones and the adults, at least, must have
heard the rumours, too. I tried to see into their hearts but I
couldn't. Because I was so uncertain, I became suspicious for no
reason. When one of the ladies dished up food for us and gave
me a little bit less than others, I thought: maybe she thinks I am
a rapist. When the other guys did not call me to join them for
soccer, I wondered: do they think I like to rape little boys?

Although no one made any remarks, I became more and
more paranoid. There were days when I did not want to see
anybody at all. After supper I'd go to my little hut and lock
myself in. I even avoided Yamkela and Atie for a while; it's hard
to explain why. It had something to do with the fact that I'd

88

been places, lived through things that others couldn't guess at. It made me feel very lonely.

Then, one evening, the Doc asked me to stay on in the living room after supper as he wanted to share a story with some of us teenagers at HOKISA. He spoke about a street kid called Mbongi, who'd had the chance to go to an excellent school to get basic skills training, but had returned after only three months to his old gang of *tikkops*. Doc asked us: 'How could he damage his own life so much? Why did he not grab this chance with both hands?'

One of the older girls said: 'It's because Mbongi does not trust anybody outside of his gang. Even if the other *tsotsis* beat him up he will keep staying with them. Because this is what he knows . . .'

We were all silent for a while. The Doc had to go somewhere and left us shortly after that. We could hear his old Toyota driving out of the parking area and disappearing into the night. Still, nobody said a word.

Then Mama Eunice, one of the childcare workers, looked at me and said softly: 'Mbu, you want to change your life, don't you?'

Until that evening I had never spoken more than three sentences in a row at HOKISA. I don't know where the sudden clarity came from, but I knew I had to speak now. I had to tell all those who were present exactly what had happened to me since my arrival at *Gogo*'s home in January: the months in prison, the proceedings at court – and my return to Masiphumelele. I talked for at least a half hour and nobody interrupted me. They all listened attentively. It felt as if a huge burden was lifted away from my shoulders.

One of the older boys said: 'We are happy that you are here now, Mbu!' Another patted me on the shoulder and said: 'Don't be late for soccer tomorrow, brother, you are a good mid-fielder . . .'

We all went to bed soon after that. Ta Simpra locked the main gate as always. '*Lala kakhuhle* – sleep well, Mbu!' he said.

*

But I did not go to sleep. I stuffed all of Mavusi's clothes into a bag and jumped over the fence. Nobody was around on this cold and windy night. I walked straight to Atie's caravan. I woke him up and asked him to join me, just for an hour or so.

One of the good things about our friendship was that Atie never asked questions. He just put on his warm sweater and followed me. He knew that I needed him badly, otherwise I would not have woken him up that late. You don't wake up a good friend for no reason.

It was not far to my mother's yard. Everyone was asleep but there was some burnt wood still glowing in one of the fire places. I took one of the sticks and blew on the glowing end. The glow became fierce orange and a little flame started to burn again.

I then emptied all of my brother's old clothes into the middle of the yard between Auntie Nompumelelo's shack and my mother's. I asked Atie for a prayer for Mavusi, for Atie and myself. He said a beautiful prayer. Then I lit the clothes with the burning stick and the wind turned all of it into a wild fire in no time. I knelt down next to the fire and cried, and called the name of my brother.

The pieces of my brother's clothing burnt down quickly. I made sure that no burning sparks were left to fly towards the shacks that could catch fire so easily, especially on stormy nights like this one.

I touched the still warm ashes with my hands. I could feel the warmth of my brother in them. The warmth of his love for me when we were both still little kids. And I knew all the time that Atie understood exactly what I was doing . . .

I took him back to his caravan and we said good night. Then I returned to HOKISA, jumping back over the fence without anybody noticing me. I slept deeply and without any dreams for the rest of that night.

*

Another two months passed. I had to study hard at school since I had missed so much in the first two terms. Once, on the weekend, I went to visit my Uncle Vukile in Ottery. He was the uncle I'd met long ago at Mavusi's funeral, whose cell number I had kept for all this time. He lived in a very poor shack in a tiny informal settlement, so small it did not even have a name. We did not speak much about my parents while I was there. But when I left, he gave me R200 – just like that! 'Be a good boy, Mbu . . .' he said to me. What a kind and generous person!

There were some weekends when I did not join Atie and Yamkela on our 'walks' as I had done in the past, because I was doing school work. But both of them remained my best friends. They never teased me about studying all by myself.

Still, I find it hard to forgive myself for the fact that on one particular Saturday evening, 23 October 2010, I once again did not join Atie and our other friends. I stayed behind in my little house, busy reading some stuff for English.

It was after ten o'clock that night when I heard some boys knocking wildly against the main gate and shouting my name: 'Mbu, Mbu, *vula* – open! Something bad has happened to your best friend!'

I ran out and opened the gate as quickly as I could. The boys were all talking at the same time and it took me a while to get the full horrible truth: a boy from another gang, Thando, had teased Atie and called his girlfriend a slut. Atie had responded by saying that the mother of Thando was the worst slut of all in Masiphumelele. That, at least, was one version. Another was that Thando had started a fight with Atie over another girl that they had both tried to get together with. Thando had been very aggressive, maybe high on drugs. But Atie, who was younger and smaller, had hit him in the face. And then . . .

About what happened next everyone agreed: Thando had pulled a knife from his pocket and without any warning, stabbed it into Atie's chest. Atie had collapsed immediately. Only then did an older neighbour intervene and call the police on his cellphone. The police arrived quickly and called the ambulance. They had just now driven off with Atie to False Bay Hospital, about ten minutes away from our township.

'And how is Atie doing?' I asked the boys anxiously.

Nobody knew. I put on my jacket, locked the gate and ran with them to the entrance to the township, hoping we might get a lift to the hospital.

When we arrived at the taxi ranks we saw a police van parked there, blue lights flashing. An officer jumped out of the car and stopped us, maybe suspecting us of fleeing the scene.

'We are friends of the boy who was attacked, and we want to go to the hospital to see him,' we told the officer.

'You're not going anywhere!' he shouted at us.

We looked at each other, knowing that nobody would stop us from going in search of Atie.

We were about to run away and take another route when we heard the policeman's walkie-talkie beeping. A voice was talking from it in Afrikaans, but all the beeps made it difficult to get the sense of what the voice was saying.

Suddenly, the noise stopped, and the policeman looked at us sadly: 'Hey boys, you don't need to go anywhere. Your friend passed away on arrival at the hospital . . .'

We all stood as if paralysed. My brain felt numb.

Atie, Atie, my best friend Atie, was dead! He was killed for nothing. Just a month before his sixteenth birthday. Atie, Atie, Atie . . .

We did not say anything to each other. Each of us walked home alone. When I turned from Pokela Road into our HOKISA road I saw a police van driving slowly towards the township entrance. I recognised Thando in the back of the car.

*

Yamkela suggested that I should write an obituary for our best friend. The funeral was two weeks later on a Saturday. His father was there and all his friends. I read the words aloud and later threw the paper into the grave, before it was filled up with sand.

It was a few days later that I asked the Doc if he would help me write a book about my life. If I could ever achieve this, I wanted to dedicate this book to Atie.

To Atie and all the many other kids like him.

A Word of Thanks
Enkosi Kakhulu

If anybody had told me a while ago that I would one day write a book about my life, I would have just laughed. Me – a writer? Who would ever be interested in anything I had to say?

When I read the books of Lutz van Dijk, one of our directors at the HOKISA Children's Home, who is called 'Doc' in my story, I was so impressed that in his books you meet ordinary young people who sometimes do unusual things. They try to change their lives, they try to care for others, they take responsibility for their future.

When I asked him whether he could help me write my story, he said: 'Are you ready to work hard for it?'

I kept quiet for a moment and he continued: 'Writing a book is hard work. Maybe you get tired after a while. Maybe you want to avoid painful or sad memories. Are you sure you're willing to work hard?'

I answered: 'Yes.'

He then asked: 'Why, Mbu? Why do you want to write your story?'

'Because I hope that other kids in trouble can learn from my life: never to give up . . . to keep on dreaming about a better future. Not to wait for others to do things for you. Never to beg. But always to learn. To work. To try to be the best person possible.'

'Okay,' he said, 'let's start.'

I admit that I did not write every chapter of this book by myself. We talked, he made notes, I brought him my notes. Then he came with a first draft. I read it and we changed it, and changed it again, until we both agreed on it.

He always said: 'This is your book, Mbu. Make sure that all is correct!' And I did. We agreed to change the names of those we could not reach to ask for permission – or those I spoke critically about and did not want to ask permission from, like *Gogo*. Sometimes we had to leave things out, as otherwise it would have been a never-ending story. But in the end, I can say: yes, this is my story. This is how I remember it. Others might remember other things.

I am still alive. Not like my best friend, Atie. Or my brother, Mavusi. Nobody will ever kill me.

I don't yet know what I will do after matric. But I want to achieve something in my life. I will never become dependent on booze or drugs. Never.

For now, I want to thank those who helped me to get where I am today.

First you, Doc. Without you, Lutz van Dijk, I would never have started this book and I would never have finished it.

Then I want to thank 'Ta Simpra' – Simphiwe Nkomombini, the leader of the HOKISA youth group. You are the best leader I have ever met in my life. Many thanks also to all the other adults and children at HOKISA. My first real home ever.

I want to thank the social workers, Karen and Nomfuneko. Because of you, I am not afraid of social workers anymore.

I want to thank my Aunt Nompumelelo. I hope one day you will believe in me again. And my uncle Vukile for being generous despite being poor – just this.

Thank you to my mother for my first school uniform.

I want to thank all my teachers, but especially 'Mrs Naki' (in real life, Mrs Ngqabi), my present teachers at Masiphumelele

High School, and the principal of Ukhanyo Primary School, Mr Thyali, and of Masiphumelele High School, Mr Mafrika. You have given me confidence that I can learn. We need many more teachers in South Africa like you.

Thank you also to my late brother Mavusi. He was the best brother one can imagine for the first few years of my life.

And above all, my gratitude goes to my best friends, Yamkela Dangisa (who will be a famous musician one day) – and Atie Rwanqa.

I will never forget you, Atie – *asoze ndiku libale.*

Mbu Maloni,
Masiphumelele,
April 2011

Photo: Chad Chapman
Yamkela Dangisa (left), Dr Lutz van Dijk and Mbu Maloni.

HOKISA Children's Home
HOKISA Ikhaya Lethu

HOKISA is a South African NGO which has been working for children and youth affected by HIV/Aids since 2001. It was founded by Karin Chubb, senior lecturer at UWC (now retired) and Dr Lutz van Dijk, German-Dutch teacher and writer.

The HOKISA Home in Masiphumelele, Cape Town, was opened on World Aids Day 2002 by Archbishop Desmond Mpilo Tutu. It is a house with a garden and a large playground, open to all township children. A second home for teenagers and young adults was built in Masiphumelele in 2005.

All royalties from this book go to Mbu Maloni to support his future training or studies.

If you want to know more about HOKISA, please visit our website: www.hokisa.co.za

We are grateful to all our friends of HOKISA in South Africa, but also in other countries like Germany, the Netherlands, Greece, Ireland, England and the USA. Donations are most welcome to the HOKISA bank account and are tax deductible in South Africa, Germany and the Netherlands.

Payee: HOKISA
Bank: Nedbank
Branch code: 104 809
Account number: 1048 052222
Swiftcode: NEDSZAJJ

Many thanks for your support!

On behalf of the HOKISA team:
    Robyn Cohen (executive director)
    Eunice Mbanjwa (senior childcare worker and team leader)

© HOKISA

World Aids Day celebration at the HOKISA Children's Home in 2003.
Mbu's best friend Atie can be seen in the first row of children (3rd
from left). Atie was eight years old when the photo was taken.

Glossary

Bakkie	Small truck.
Buthi	Brother.
Chicks	Slang for 'girls'.
Dagga	Marijuana.
Domestic	Housemaid.
Ewe	Yes.
Haybo	Exclamation of surprise or disapproval.
Hayi	No.
Lekker	Nice.
Makazi	Aunt.
Masizakhe	Literally: 'Let us Build'.
Matric	Short for Matriculation, the final school-leaving year.
Mealie	Maize.
Moffie	Derogatory slang for someone who is homosexual.

Molo	A greeting to one person.
Molweni	A greeting to more than one person.
RDP house	Low-cost housing built by the government as part of the Reconstruction and Development Programme.
Shebeen	Informal drinking den.
Sisi	Sister.
Spaza	Informal sector shop selling small goods.
Tata	Father.
Tik	A cheap drug that damages the brain and can lead to aggressive behaviour.
Tikkop	Literally, 'Tik head'; someone who uses Tik.
Tsotsi	Street criminal.
Vrygrond	Afrikaans for 'Free Ground'.